T0178752

Decision-making in Crisis Situations

Series Editor
Jean-Charles Pomerol

Decision-making in Crisis Situations

*Research and Innovation
for Optimal Training*

Edited by

Sophie Sauvagnargues

WILEY

First published 2018 in Great Britain and the United States by ISTE Ltd and John Wiley & Sons, Inc.

ISTE Ltd
27–37 St George's Road
London SW19 4EU
UK

www.iste.co.uk

John Wiley & Sons, Inc.
111 River Street
Hoboken, NJ 07030
USA

www.wiley.com

Library of Congress Control Number: 2018953112

British Library Cataloguing-in-Publication Data
A CIP record for this book is available from the British Library
ISBN 978-1-78630-343-1

Contents

Philippe LIMOUSIN, Aurélia BONY-DANDRIEUX, Jérôme TIXIER and
Sophie SAUVAGNARGUES

Noémie FRÉALLE, Florian TENA-CHOLLET and Sophie SAUVAGNARGUES

Dimitri LAPIERRE, Florian TENA-CHOLLET, Jérôme TIXIER,
Aurélia BONY-DANDRIEUX and Karine WEISS

David GOUTX, Sophie SAUVAGNARGUES and Laurent MERMET

Clément LAVERDET, Karine WEISS, Aurélia BONY-DANDRIEUX,
Jérôme TIXIER and Serge CAPAROS

Sophie SAUVAGNARGUES, Dimitri LAPIERRE, Philippe LIMOUSIN,
Noémie FRÉALLE, Florian TENA-CHOLLET, David GOUTX,
Pierre-Alain AYRAL, Aurélia BONY-DANDRIEUX and Jérôme TIXIER

Introduction

Whether environmental, economic, social, health or humanitarian, a crisis is a complex phenomenon that requires a management strategy specific to each situation. A crisis arises after a sudden and unexpected triggering event, and is characterized by rapid changes that require optimal cooperation between various participants who are faced with a stressful situation. How the crisis is managed impacts how it unfolds.

It is therefore a matter of anticipating events and making decisions, most of which are urgent and crucial, and may need to be made on the basis of contradictory requirements, while facing a context of structural disruption. The complexities of managing a crisis situation can be seen as "a set of factors aimed at combating crises and reducing the actual damage suffered, while aiming to prevent or mitigate the negative effects of the crisis and protect the organisation, managers and/or the industrialist" (Coombs *et al.* 2010).

Decisions are made at different levels: the *strategic level* corresponds to the description of the aims and objectives set in order to deal with the crisis and concerns the decision-making structures; the *tactical level* is linked to the organization of field operations with a view to implementing the strategies drawn up; and the *operational level* executes and implements the resources relating to the organization of field operations. The crisis unit is thus the central

Chapter written by Sophie SAUVAGNARGUES.

instrument in the strategic management of the crisis, essential to any organization. It is both an open place because it is at the crossroads of information and its processing and decision-making, and a closed place which must allow the cell to function without disruption (Heiderich 2010).

In the field of major risks, a strategic crisis unit can be municipal, departmental, prefectoral, national or that of an industrial company. It unites human resources, computing and communication resources, individual or collective equipment and specific documentation relating to emergency management.

The realization of the missions assigned to a crisis unit, and anticipating and making decisions, requires a multitude of competences. Flück's model (Flück 2001) proposes four types of combined skills to react to the different professional situations encountered: technical skills (theoretical knowledge and trades, methods and tools, rules and procedures, know-how linked to experience), organizational skills (spatio-temporal organization and management of information flows), relational and social skills (oral and written expression skills, interpersonal skills, managerial and network skills) and adaptation skills (ability to adjust to the situation and its evolution over time and to transfer acquired know-how).

The acquisition and preservation of these skills is complex, all the more so when, outside of a crisis situation, it is not the main goal or function of the people concerned. The crisis unit is subject to high levels of stress as well as to various biases impacting its members in their representation and decision-making. The difficulties encountered by decision-makers in crisis cells in terms of decision-making and collective behavior necessitate training exercises to prepare them to face this type of situation. "The implementation of simulation exercises, the development of crisis scenarios outside the framework, the coordination of an even greater number of actors as well as a real line of conduct for crisis units, priorities in crisis management and in particular in terms of training are at the heart of concerns" (Lagadec 2012).

The purpose of this book is to specifically focus on decision-making training through crisis simulation. The aim is essentially educational, methodological and practical, and provides a concise review of the major knowledge, methods and innovative tools in this field.

This book is composed of eight chapters:

– The first chapter, "Concepts, Tools and Methods for Crisis Management Training", provides an overview of the problem of crisis management training. The authors present the characteristics of the crisis unit before discussing the various aspects of crisis management training, including stress simulations, in detail.

– The second chapter, "Towards A Serious Game Within the Frame of Major Crisis Simulations for Decision-makers: How Do We Connect the DOTs?", proposes the development of a semi-virtual training environment to ensure effective learning, mainly through improved experience, engagement and immersion, and realism. Degrees Of Training (DOTs) are organized into general, intermediate and specific skills to be involved in each crisis scenario.

– The third chapter, "Improving Crisis Exercises and Managers' Skills through the Development of Scenario Design", discusses the interest in improving the scripting phase of an exercise model in order to improve crisis management training and experiential learning.

– The fourth chapter, "Elaboration of Tools to Facilitate the Scenario Development of Crisis Management Training", discusses how to develop a scenario which is credible, educational and interactive, so as to encourage trainees to be immersed in a situation which seems realistic and that allows them to acquire knowledge, skills and experience.

– The fifth chapter, "How Can We Evaluate the Participants of a Crisis Management Training Exercise", presents an innovative methodology of evaluation and debriefing facilitation, resulting from the observation of the limits of the current training in evaluation and debriefing.

– The sixth chapter, "Managing the Game Within Crisis Exercises", focuses on the playful dynamics at work when a group of trainees agree to consider seriously, for a few hours, that they will together role-play a virtual crisis situation. It particularly takes into account the key components of Ludicity, the manifestations of Ludicity, and how to manage Ludicity.

– The seventh chapter, "Digital Training for Authorities: What is the Best Way to Communicate During a Crisis?", proposes to standardize some of the analyses performed on crisis management to produce a comprehensive report on the quality of the crisis communication delivered. This report may be produced following a real situation or during an emergency response drill.

– Finally, the eighth chapter, "Some Perspectives Moving Forward", offers perspectives and development paths, in terms of realistic simulation of crisis scenarios and optimization of the didactic processes involved and of the tools implemented.

I.1. References

Coombs, W.T., Holladay, S.J., and Thompson, B. (2010). *The Handbook of Crisis Communication*. Blackwell, Hoboken.

Heiderich, D. (2010). *Plan de gestion de crise : organiser, gérer et communiquer en situation de crise*. Dunod, Paris.

Flück, C. (2001). *Compétences et performances, une alliance réussie*. Demos, Paris.

Lagadec, P. (2012). *Du risque majeur aux mégachocs*. Préventique, Bordeaux.

Concepts, Tools and Methods for Crisis Management Training

The purpose of this chapter is to provide an overview of the field of crisis management training. As a first step, the descriptive elements of the crisis unit will make it possible to delineate the characteristics of this top decision-making place. Then, the different aspects of crisis management training will be addressed, before thoroughly introducing the concept of crisis simulations, which are one of the specific forms that trainings may adopt. Simulations are built and characterized by scenarios which materialize the training goals and educational content and thus favor a relevant organizational learning process. Finally, in order to illustrate the overview of this problem, we will portray the simulation and research platform of the French Institute of Risk Sciences (IMT Mines Alès).

1.1. The crisis unit at the heart of the process

The crisis team reunites decision makers who face a critical situation in a single place.

A crisis unit can be defined as a team with strong organizational integration (Sundstrom *et al.* 1990), in which different roles and

Chapter written by Sophie SAUVAGNARGUES, Dimitri LAPIERRE, Philippe LIMOUSIN, Noémie FRÉALLE, Florian TENA-CHOLLET, Pierre-Alain AYRAL, Aurélia BONY-DANDRIEUX and Jérôme TIXIER.

responsibilities are finely structured (Salas *et al.* 1992) and hierarchized (Ahlstrom *et al.* 2000; Vraie *et al.* 2010). The members of the crisis unit are mobilized because of their skills and knowledge, and share a frame of reference and procedures (Ahlström *et al.* 2000) in order to accomplish the missions entrusted to them (Lachtar 2012). Considering that the activation of a crisis unit depends on the occurrence of an event requiring its mobilization, it is actually an ephemeral organization (Dautun and Lacroix 2013; MAEE 2017).

This top decision-making place, which, by definition, must suddenly be ready for operations, can quickly assume the features of a bunker, in order to accomplish its function for centralizing the various members of the organization (Maisonneuve 2010). However, it is essential that its members do not perceive the crisis room as a bunker (Lagadec 1995, 2012), so as to avoid the harmful effects of confinement on the decision-making process.

Human behavior, whether individual or collective, is at the core of a crisis unit's life (Guzzo *et al.* 1995; Marks *et al.* 2001; Weil *et al.* 2004; Hussain *et al.* 2007). Beyond the achievement of specific tasks, behavioral processes occupy a prominent place in the functioning of the crisis unit (Shanahan *et al.* 2007), particularly in regard to coordination, cooperation and communication mechanisms between members. In an emergency, the decision-making process is complex because the crisis unit is exposed to high levels of stress (highly challenging decisions, hierarchical or media pressure, etc.), as well as different prejudices, which may have an impact on its members, their representations and their decisions. During the acute phase of a crisis, it seems that policymakers prefer procedural (Crichton 2000; O'Connor and Dea 2007; Lagadec 2012), intuitive (Klein 1997; Lagadec and Guilhou 2002a,b) and creative (Crichton 2000; O'Connor and Dea 2007) decision-making, in the measure that their experience and the unpredictability of the crisis increase (Lapierre 2016).

Therefore, training exercises can prepare crisis unit decision makers for the complexity of these unstable universes, and help them to deal with the obstacles encountered during a critical situation, regardless of whether these are individual difficulties or collective dysfunctions.

Collective dysfunctions mainly concern the transmission of information within the crisis unit, as well as among the actors involved, particularly on how they understand the situation and cope with stress and organizational aspects. They have a direct impact on decision-making and an indirect one on the whole of the organization. These dysfunctions can be classified according to the categories presented in Table 1.1.

Problems related to the transmission of information	References
Weak information sharing	King *et al.* (2008)
Improper information transmission: omissions, inaccuracies, lack of clarity, etc.	Crichton and Flin (2004), Guarnieri *et al.* (2016), Guarnieri *et al.* (2015)
Selectivity in the information chosen, oversight of other relevant data	Kowalski-Trakofler and Vaught (2003), Guarnieri *et al.* (2015)
Lack of validation, decision control	Guarnieri *et al.* (2015)
Dysfunctions related to the situation	
Insufficient knowledge about the event and the stakes involved	Dautun (2007)
Difficulty to obtain a common operating picture, a common mental representation	Seppänen *et al.* (2013), Lagadec (2015)
Collapse of sense ("sense-making")	Weick (1995)
Control fantasy	Kouabenan *et al.* (2006)
Misrepresentation of risk, normalization of deviance	Vaughan (1996)
Effects of "groupthink" on the crisis unit	Guarnieri *et al.* (2015)
Lack of perspective on the situation	Lagadec and Guilhou (2002a,b)
Negation of the unexpected	Lagadec (2012)
Inadequate or erroneous assessment of the situation	Crichton and Flin (2004), Guarnieri *et al.* (2015), Orasanu (2010)

Misunderstanding in the face of inconsistent, inadequate or unfeasible demands	Guarnieri *et al.* (2015)
Dysfunctions related to stress	
Denial, voluntary blindness, negation of the unexpected	Kouabenan *et al.* (2006), Lagadec (2010), Heiderich (2010), Lagadec (2012)
Blocking action, ineffective processing of information	Kouabenan *et al.* (2006), Combalbert and Delbecque (2012)
Feeling of invulnerability	Kouabenan *et al.* (2006)
Consternation	Crocq *et al.* (2009)
Disorientation of members	Heiderich (2010)
Decrease in alertness and memory capabilities	Kontogiannis and Kossiavelou (1999)
Need to find/appoint leaders, instead of becoming involved	Wybo (2009)
Ignorance, beliefs, ideology, arrogance and intellectual misrepresentation	Lagadec (2010), Heiderich (2010), Lagadec (2012)
Organizational dysfunctions	
Partial implementation or difficulty of setting up the cell	Dautun (2007)
Lack of available resources	Guarnieri *et al.* (2015)
Lack of reflexes, or bad reflexes	Suchet (2015)
Ambiguity of roles	Moulin (2014)
Incorrect distribution of tasks, lack of (or bad pooling of) resources	Kanki (2010)
Blind endorsement or misapplication of procedures	Crichton and Flin (2004), Lagadec (2012)
Weak leadership	Kanki (2010), Moulin (2014)
Disobedience to the leader	Guarnieri *et al.* (2015)
Tensions, conflicts, lack of cohesion	Van Vliet and van Amelsfoort (2008), Argillos (2004)
Lack of consensus	Denis (1993)

Collapse or lack of coordination devices	Weick (1995), Lagadec (2012), Kim *et al.* (2015), Smith and Dowell (2000)
Lack of support from the leaders, excessive hierarchical pressure	Guarnieri *et al.* (2015)
Lack of deep personal knowledge and of other players	Moulin (2014)
Isolation and confinement of crisis unit members	Guarnieri *et al.* (2015)
Lack of adaptability, difficulty to innovate, improvise or reorganize oneself	Edmond (2011), Autissier *et al.* (2012)
Lack of anticipation	Lagadec and Guilhou (2002a,b)
Dysfunctions associated with external crisis communication	
Absence or lack of external communication to the cell	Lagadec (1995)
Difficult or inappropriate communication with the outside	Dautun (2007); Kim *et al.* (2015)

Table 1.1. *Collective dysfunctions that may emerge at the crisis unit (according to Lapierre (2016) and Limousin (2017))*

These difficulties and shortcomings show the importance of the human factor for crisis management. On the other hand, during critical situations, managers are confronted with other complications such as the lack of technical or human resources (Lagadec 2010, Guarnieri *et al.* 2016), incompleteness, the lack of updates and the inadequacy of emergency plans to face the situation (Dautun 2007; Cesta *et al.* 2014).

All of these elements have a hindering effect on the adequate management of a critical situation. Hence, there is a need for upstream training in order to avoid them, or at least to reduce their potential consequences.

1.2. Training for crisis units

In order to prepare the crisis tool and make it efficient, it is necessary to raise awareness about it, test it out and constantly improve it (Solucom 2014).

Training sessions in the field of major risk and crisis management are essential for the actors involved in the crisis. Training comprises all of the theoretical lessons (learning) and drills (practicing) that make it possible to prepare oneself and to perfect one's skills (Quinton 2007). Training also contributes to increasing the readiness level of managers and highlights the functional, technical and organizational problems inherent in crisis management (Renaudin and Altemaire 2007).

Training sessions may cover several objectives, in particular to:

–test documentation, plans, procedures and the operational capability of crisis management tools (Gaultier *et al.* 2012);

–highlight dysfunctions and the areas to be improved (Heiderich 2010);

–encourage the crisis members to gain experience (Sayegh *et al.* 2004; Tissigton and Flin 2005);

–test the efficiency of mobilized staff (Gaultier-Gaillard *et al.* 2012);

–raise the level of expertise of the actors involved (Crichton 2001).

The skills that should be developed by managers are manifold. On another note, the dysfunctions previously identified in the crisis units highlight the need to insist on several criteria during the training sessions:

–Reflection in the middle of an emergency: an emergency is typical during the acute phase of a crisis; therefore, it must be integrated in training scenarios. It is necessary to generate stressful situations within the frame of exercise scenarios in view of imposing quick thinking to decision makers while destabilizing their organization.

–Group: training should focus on the reactions and behavior of the group as a whole, and not on individuals, relying on the fundamental skills of the trained group (decision-making, communication, situational awareness, leadership, coordination).

–Objectives: group learning should be at the heart of the approach. Promoting exercises in strenuous conditions also contributes to the characterization of individual and collective goals throughout the training.

–Learning the surprise element and anticipating disruption (Roux-Dufort and Ramboatiana 2006).

At present, there are many types of trainings, which may vary strongly (Bapst and Gaspar 2011). Stern and Hedstrom have tried to find consensus as regards training terminology (Stern 2014). The first distinction is the fact that training can be theoretical or practical. The second one focuses on the difference between courses for developing skills and those which help members to put these skills into action.

On another note, it is possible to distinguish between education, functional exercise, training and courses:

–Education is defined as a training program designed to increase the knowledge or understanding of a topic. Education is opposite to training for improving skills related to a specific task (Department of Homeland Security FEMA, 2015).

–A functional exercise is a commonly practiced activity in order to test a single and specific operation or the function of an entity (Blanchard 2008).

–Training is a coordinated and supervised action which is usually performed in view of validating an operation or a specific function within an organization. Training is performed in order to become used to new equipment, to develop or test new procedures or to maintain acquired skills (Department of Homeland Security of FEMA 2005).

–Courses correspond to activities which have been scheduled in order to improve the effectiveness of individuals and organizations (Blanchard 2008).

A classification has been proposed by the HSEEP (Homeland Security Exercise and Evaluation Program) for the totality of crisis management trainings. These are classified according to the required skills, necessary preparation and upstream training (Lee *et al.* 2006) so as to reach different educational levels:

–The seminar helps trainees to obtain a general overview of crisis management. For this purpose, authorities, strategies, plans and regulations can be introduced. Besides, seminars are a good tool to raise awareness about crisis management (Department of Homeland Security of FEMA 2013).

–If the goals are initially well defined, then workshops can favor the achievement of a concrete result (procedure, protocol, concept). It is appropriate to propose workshops to crisis management actors, because this enables them to later include what has been produced by their work (Department of Homeland Security of FEMA 2013).

–Tabletop exercises are intended to spark discussions regarding a simulated emergency within a caring framework. If trainees become engaged in these exercises, awareness and the understanding of concepts and/or procedures are effective (Tena-Chollet 2012; Department of Homeland Security of FEMA 2013).

–Games are simulations of operations which enable trainees to explore plans or processes. The format of the game and its rules is open, in order to experience some aspects in real time or to linger on the decision-making process (Department of Homeland Security of FEMA 2013). Games also help participants to explore the decision-making processes resulting from plans, by exploring their consequences (Renger *et al.* 2009).

–Practical exercises are tests in which only one operation or function is evaluated. Exercises are simulated in real time and can last 2 to 4 hours (Federal Emergency Management Agency 2008).

–Functional exercises are conducted in real time and in the usual crisis management environment (Tena-Chollet 2012; Department of Homeland Security of FEMA 2013). They do not address all of the functions of crisis management and limit the movements of staff and equipment, which are consequently simulated (Tena-Chollet 2012; Department of Homeland Security of FEMA 2013).

–Large-scale exercises can be considered as the most ambitious ones (DDSC 2005), in virtue of their complex preparation and the significant resources they require in order to reliably reproduce an event (Department of Homeland Security of FEMA 2013). They involve a large number of stakeholders who can identify problems (including cooperation among different departments) and then adjust the procedures that must be followed (Tena-Chollet 2012; Department of Homeland Security of FEMA 2013).

We can complete this classification with serious games, defined as "a computer application, whose initial intention is to consistently combine serious aspects, such as education, learning, communication, or information, with playful proposals derived from video games (games). Such an association can take place thanks to the implementation of a 'utility scenario', that is to say, a special presentation (with sounds and graphs), including a script as well as appropriate rules, whose intention from the very beginning is to go beyond simple entertainment" (Alvarez 2007). Serious games can be classified into three categories (Lhuillier 2011):

–*Learning games* are serious games for learning or training, with the main goal of providing training to enhance the acquisition of skills and knowledge.

–*Persuasive games* are used for communicating informative, persuasive (institutional communication, advertising, etc.) or subjective (propaganda) messages. Their goals are to seduce, promote, influence and persuade.

–Simulations are used for training players in the acquisition of reflexes. Thus, the trainee can repeat and reproduce certain gestures or procedures and perfect them.

The training offer is rich, as shown in Figure 1.1 (Fréalle 2018). It is also important to choose training activities in a consistent manner, that is, in harmony with the educational goals and the predetermined training scenario. It is also essential for the trainer to adapt to trainees, in order to improve the quality of the learning experience

(Bristow *et al.* 2011). Finally, training in crisis management should be an immersive experience based on real events, and truthfully reflect the discussion on the causes, consequences, prevention and management of crises (Shrivastava *et al.* 2012).

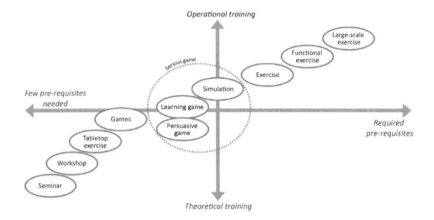

Figure 1.1. *A summary of the different types of training that can be used for crisis management training (Fréalle 2018). For a color version of this figure, see www.iste.co.uk/sauvagnargues/crisis.zip*

1.3. Simulation of critical situations

Here, attention is focused on successful simulations so that trainees can integrate knowledge (Miles *et al.* 1986 and Jennings 2002 in Goebel and Humphreys 2014). Simulation allows trainees to simulate reality and acquire a type of experience which may be perceived as a rite of passage (Goutx 2014). It is necessary to make sure that the training, and most importantly the simulation, will help organizers reach educational goals and thus improve organizational resiliency.

The use of simulation is becoming increasingly widespread in the learning process (Pernin 1996; Mellet d'Huart 2001; Pastré 2005). The main practical reasons underlying the interest in the use of simulation have been studied by many authors (Crichton *et al.* 2000; Banks 2001; Lourdeaux 2001; Borodzicz *et al.* 2002; Querrec 2002; Guéraud 2003; Kincaid *et al.* 2003; Guéraud 2005; Bruinsma and De Hoog 2006; Idasiak *et al.* 2006; Joab *et al.* 2006; Mendonca *et al.* 2006;

Schurr *et al.* 2006; Crichton 2009). The interest of simulation can be defined through:

–the potential danger to humans, the environment or the equipment when working on the real system (risky or situations difficult to reproduce);

–the source of anxiety that the real system may represent for a beginner;

–the ability to simulate extremely severe situations to prepare the trainee to respond to them;

–the freedom from the constraint of a time scale which may ease understanding;

–the opportunity to simplify or alter a reality in order to study it better;

–the acquisition of skills related to decision-making and problem-solving;

–the interest for the trainee; since simulation can act as a source of motivation, it can contribute to a better understanding of phenomena and a greater ability to become adapted in similar situations;

–training costs which are lower, regardless of whether they are related to financial issues or problems concerning the mobilization of staff.

By definition, a simulator is "a dynamic technical and human environment, endowed with interactive points which the operator may manipulate in order to cause, observe or control changes in this environment" (Crampes and Saussac 1999). The purpose of this type of tool is to learn technical and non-technical skills, know-how and reflective practices. For this purpose, a simulator is supposed to integrate parameters such as realism, time and the stakes involved, in order to favor the complete immersion of the participant. The temporal component can be divided into two categories: real time for simulations taking place within the same temporal space as the real and simulated time, which corresponds to an acceleration or deceleration in real time (Crampes and Saussac 1998). Pernin identifies three contexts in which simulations are used (Pernin 1996):

–the traditional context in which the pedagogue resorts to simulation for demonstrative purposes, or suggests activities related to simulation. His role is to guide and help trainees;

–an independent use, as part of self-training or self-assessment;

–cooperative use in the context of a group of trainees doing cooperative work based on simulation.

We should observe that the use of simulators is spreading in different contexts and training frameworks. Various works tend to explain their effectiveness in learning through fixed educational goals, a set of rules particularly defined for the trainee and the guidance offered by facilitators (Pernin 1996; Cortes Buitrago 1999). In this way, in educational simulators, the trainee is placed in a learning situation through discovery and action (Pernin 1996; Joab et al. 2006; Labat et al. 2006). The main intention for using educational simulation is to favor the learning process, which is not necessarily related to the accuracy of the modeling of the simulated system (Cortes Buitrago 1999; Crampes and Saussac 1999; Joab et al. 2006). Hence, a pedagogical simulation designer is free to simplify or highlight specific phenomena or some features of the simulated system when these differences are justified from a pedagogical point of view. Exercises are usually supervised by one or more trainers (Joab et al. 2006), and didactic interventions must be defined according to several criteria. In fact, each event scenario depends on the profile of the trainee and the type of error he tends to make (Lourdeaux 2001). In general, the more the trained individual is confirmed, the better it is to make him aware of his mistake, without taking him out of the simulated situation.

In the design of a simulator for educational purposes, it is important to define the different teaching strategies from the beginning. These may include the following elements: the motivation process (stakes, competition, emergency, etc.), a performance evaluation, the way in which knowledge will be brought forward and, finally, the way in which the trainee will acquire experience. Realism is an important element, but it has nonetheless been proven that it should leave room for imagination so that trainees can take ownership of the situation (Crampes and Saussac 1999). According to the proposed training and the goal set, participants can play one or many different roles during the same training.

Visualization is also one of the key elements involved in simulation, given the fact that since childhood, the human brain has been used to primarily focus on the visual aspect of things (Rohrer 2000). In order to improve the process of human understanding, different sources of information can be made accessible and should be chosen on the basis of the message that must be conveyed (Morin *et al.* 2004):

–visual aims, which can be adapted so that teams can feel motivated;

–maps, which can be dedicated to monitoring of the situation and illustrating the geographical limits of the simulation territory;

–statistics, which can enable the synthesis of a large amount of data;

–temporal trends, which can foster the perception of changes in the simulated system;

–photographs, which can statically illustrate a situation;

–2D or 3D animations, which can properly reflect the dynamics of events.

The benefits associated with the use of simulation for educational purposes are manifold (Banks 2000). First, it is possible to test the simulation parameters and validate them (or not). It is also possible to understand why an event takes place in one way or another, by studying it in retrospect and exploring different evolutions of the simulated scenario, in order to learn from previous mistakes without risking real-life consequences (Mendonca *et al.* 2006).

However, simulation also presents some drawbacks related to the difficulty of representing results (transcription problem) and the assessment of team performance (interpretation problem). This stems from the fact that the impact of decisions made by the group regarding the evolution of simulation is not often observable or is difficult to measure (Banks 2000).

It is therefore necessary to reflect upon the strategies that must be integrated so as to improve the collective learning of participants. For this purpose, different levers should be considered, such as a better characterization of needs and expectations from trainees, and a better appraisal of the non-technical skills of a group, associated with the enrichment of learning environments.

1.4. The construction of crisis simulation exercises

A better consideration of non-technical skills initially requires a precise identification of the training exercise goals (Salas and Cannon-Bowers 2001; Bernard 2014). An analysis of the tasks (or actions) that must be achieved needs to be conducted before the exercise; that is, it should characterize the expectations related to scheduled tasks. A cognitive task analysis can be performed by the designers of the training. Before the exercise, this technique explores the skills that will be needed by trainees in order to perform the task (abilities, association of ideas, existing rules or procedures). This will allow educators to improve the design of scenarios, by incorporating more of the trainees' needs. On the other hand, once these various elements have been identified, the technique makes it possible to easily translate such needs into learning objectives and later transcribe them within the scenario construction phase.

In fact, when a crisis occurs, non-technical skills, and specifically psycho-social factors, are generally lacking. The crisis takes place under psychological strain, whether at the individual or collective level, because the time of the crisis is an accelerated time, rushed, in which things are going too fast in the minds of the individuals (Crocq et al. 2009). Individuals who experience the crisis think that they are no longer able to control events as the situation goes far beyond their reach. They are obliged to suddenly change their habits and undergo a sole life-saving imperative, to effectively make a decision in a very short time lapse. The preparation of decision makers through training rarely meets these criteria (Pearson and Clair 1998).

Fear, anxiety, anguish and stress, which have an impact on decision-making, modify the group dynamics and the representation of the situation (Heiderich 2010), which are all examples of appropriate or inappropriate reactions on the part of managers in the middle of the emergency (Crocq 2007; Dautun 2007). However, during training, it is very difficult to inject the stimuli of fear, anxiety or stress due to the exercise context. NASA designs exercises in which the fatigue factor is predominant, in order to evaluate the decision-making abilities of staff. This type of training is rare in other areas (Helmreich *et al.* 1986).

In order to increase the recognition of these aspects, several authors have suggested that more emphasis should be placed on transmitting the informal rules which are at work during critical situations to decision makers and operators (Llory 1996). Recommendations or simple practical rules can be proposed to train decision makers during the course: among these recommendations, some can be mentioned, particularly in view of strengthening the enforcement of procedures and of reducing associated errors which often occur when hasty decisions are made. For example, in case of doubt, it is recommended to double-check information. This principle also applies when the different stages of a procedure must be respected. It should be emphasized that some of these should not be forgotten, even in the context of a crisis (Llory 1996).

Finally, other authors have emphasized the importance of some skills that are essential for all organizations, but often overlooked (Lagadec 2012): for a long time, exercises have focused on procedures to be applied, instead of the human or organizational factor. The same applies to oral communication: specific learning activities should focus on some particular skills (Seppänen *et al.* 2013), such as making people speak one after the other, generating actions that can only be achieved with the joint efforts of many or working on the type of information exchanged. Training participants on how to communicate among members in unfavorable conditions (Quarantelli 1988), simulating media pressure, varying the different channels for disseminating information (Becerra *et al.* 2013) or considering the impact of social networks in managing emergencies (particularly, Social Media in Emergency Management – SMEM) are part of these recommendations (Martin 2014).

In addition to the major dysfunctions that a crisis unit may have to meet, the importance of the working habits of decision makers, as well as their initial thinking environment, should also be reconsidered.

Organizational learning takes place by activating levers at different moments within a training schedule, all the more considering that improvement is possible at all levels: in the context of a (real or simulated) crisis, an emergency deprives decision makers from deep knowledge of the situation and thus becomes one of the first areas to be improved. It is therefore necessary to educate trainees to embark upon an information-sharing process.

The elements regarding the development of a shared awareness on the situation should be strengthened during the training exercise. In fact, shared mental models shape a common understanding of the situation among the group members, a comprehension that is essential during a critical situation. Without a common operational picture and knowledge of the roles and missions of each participant, shared awareness of the situation may be low in the crisis unit, which can have a negative impact on the decision-making process (Seppänen *et al.* 2013).

Operational mapping is a major component of a shared awareness of the critical situation. It helps to (graphically and dynamically) outline important shared information concerning the crisis, as well as to secure and optimize the collection, transmission and understanding of operational information at different commanding levels (Sauvagnargues and Poppi 2012).

On the other hand, four team-working processes are at the heart of such a construction to overcome collective failure (Dautun and Lacroix 2013):

–Interpersonal communication: reformulating common terms, encouraging strong interaction between members, favoring an effective flow of information. In other words, raising awareness about closed-loop communication (Henriksen *et al.* 2008).

–Coordination: gathering and assembling evidence to shape a shared vision through the drafting of action, carrying out regular check-ups.

–Cooperation: mutual trust among members implies strong cooperation.

–Use of shared tools: when deprived of a vision of reality, members must create a mental image of the crisis. Therefore, this requires a high level of assistance for sharing information and effectively managing the situation. Some examples of supporting media are mapping, tracking charts and records (Lagadec 2012; Lachtar 2012).

In other words, in order to improve the quality of the learning environment, and from a material point of view, it is necessary for the places destined for training to be equipped with tools to enable trainees to share information with the whole group. The goal is to transform this approach into a reflex and to enable the group members to develop a habit.

The enrichment of the environment lies at the heart of developing a training exercise in order to create an optimal learning atmosphere: trainees should be placed in a situation that highlights their experience through "target" events, as well as expected actions and behaviors. Scenarios must be finely scripted, without nonetheless becoming rigid, which might endanger their flexibility during training (Boin *et al.* 2004). In one scenario, an event is never trivial, and goals, missions, actions or expectations need to be deduced beforehand (Shapiro *et al.* 2008).

Scenarios should ideally be based on the objectives, particularly on clearly identified educational goals, a realistic story, missions to be attained, distinct roles, specific operations and varied resources (Schank *et al.* 1992). When a scenario is well structured and trainees feel immersed in it, their motivation is positively impacted. This immersion is directly related to the environment and the exercise scenario. Many authors have pointed out that in order to favor involvement, an exercise should imperatively respect the accuracy triangle (Rehmann *et al.* 1995; Powers *et al.* 2013):

–physical aspect of the simulator: true to life equipment;

–environmental aspect of the simulator: derelict environment;

–feeling of immersion among trainees.

In order to enhance organizational learning, through the different scenarios, it is therefore convenient to elicit several distinct skills, alternate them, make changes and fluctuate the level of difficulty during the exercise (Salas and Cannon-Bowers 2001), involving a variety of institutional actors and State services related to civil security (Lagadec and Guilhou 2002b; Lagadec 2012), especially considering elements which are not spontaneously given.

The heart of a simulation is its scenario (Nissen 2009; Hotte 2016). It is necessary to understand the scriptwriting mechanics employed, so as to evaluate whether the scenario favors the achievement of educational ambitions related to learning.

The scenario of crisis management training is the story of how the future could develop (Heinzen 1995; Carroll 2000; Noori *et al.* 2017). The scenario designed for a simulation describes a single event or a hypothetical situation in a relatively short time frame, ranging from a few hours to a few days (Heinzen 1995). It is the tool that provides the participant with the necessary training experience so as to develop effectiveness during critical situations, by creating a feeling of *flow* (Csikszentmihalyi 1991) and immersion (Heinzen 1995; Lukosch *et al.* 2012).

Apart from being stimulating (Noori *et al.* 2017), the scenario should faithfully reflect reality so that learning is relevant (Dautun *et al.* 2011; Pastré and Vergnaud 2011), flexible and dynamic (Dautun *et al.* 2011; Noori *et al.* 2017). These characteristics can be structured through three prerequisites: the scenario must be credible, educational and interactive. A true-to-life scenario will be a credible scenario; a scenario favoring the acquisition or consolidation of knowledge, skills and know-how will be a pedagogical scenario; a scenario enriched with interactivity will be a flexible and dynamic scenario. To be sure that the simulation is carried out in coherence with the prerequisites, the scripting stage should take these characteristics into account.

1.5. The simulation and research platform of the Institute of Risk Sciences (IMT Mines Alès)

The simulation platform was built in 2011. It is a research platform in which it is possible to develop and test different devices, to immerse trainees in crisis situations, isolating them in a room representing a crisis unit. The simulation platform is composed of four rooms, which are distributed as follows (Figure 1.2):

–two rooms for trainees. It is therefore possible to separate trainees into two groups and to develop the same scenario in parallel. We can also consider forming two different crisis units and implementing a self-powered scenario;

–a room for facilitators, which is located in the heart of the simulation platform;

–the technical platform of the simulation room.

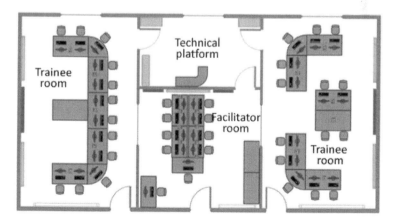

Figure 1.2. *A diagram of the simulation platform. For a color version of this figure, see www.iste.co.uk/sauvagnargues/crisis.zip*

We can classify the facilities of this platform into three categories:

–The equipment available to trainees. These are facilities found in crisis units, and if they are crisis managers, they enable trainees to be placed in conditions similar to the ones that their organization may face. This may contribute to helping trainees become familiar with equipment which may not be readily available in their structure of origin. Rooms for trainees are equipped with an interactive whiteboard (IWB), a wall screen, a large touch screen, a flip chart, a whiteboard, billboards, a printer, a computer station and one phone per person.

–All this equipment enables educators to control the simulation. Thus, trainees can have access to surveillance cameras, a remote control of the trainees' screens (IWB, screen wall, touch screen), control of the trainee room's sound system, a printer, a computer station and one phone per person, an IWB, a whiteboard and billboards. One-way windows between rooms where trainees are located and the animation room enable facilitators to have direct visual access to trainees.

–Sound, visual and thermal immersion equipment for trainees. This equipment facilitates the engagement of trainees in the learning situation: obscuring shutters make it possible to avoid what is happening outside (which might discredit the simulation), the room's thermostat can be regulated and thanks to the sound system, it is possible to submit relevant sound elements related to the simulated situation to trainees.

This experimentation platform helps to control simulation settings at the best possible level. In fact, it is possible to choose the devices made available to trainees and facilitators as well as to determine the spatial organization of the crisis unit. In the way it has been introduced here, the simulator offers two configurations, a reflection of the majority of documented crisis units:

–"U-shaped" configuration: this facilitates coordination between the different poles, the transmission of information and the visibility of points of interest (whiteboard, flipchart, records, mapping, etc.).

–Island configuration: this facilitates work in small groups and movement of the members in the crisis unit, a feature that improves access to shared media (white tables, paperboard, records, mapping, etc.).

Implemented simulations make it possible to prepare trainees for participation in a crisis unit, by exposing them to the various obstacles and difficulties that may be encountered in these uncertain contexts. Dysfunctions, essentially collective ones, highlighted in crisis units (and described in section 1.1), are considered as reflection matter for the construction of scenarios.

Each simulation training session is subjected to the precise definition of educational goals, specially adapted to the training audience (institutional, local authorities, industrial, students). Trainings sessions are intended to promote reflection in the middle of an emergency and to provoke reactions and group behavior for decision-making, coordination, representation and shaping the collective consciousness of the situation, leadership, etc.

After the precise definition of educational objectives, each scenario is "tailor-made" for each group of trainees, whether in terms of:

–the considered triggering phenomenon (flooding, accident during the transport of hazardous materials, forest fires, hurricanes, etc.);

–the type of crisis unit deployed (communal, industrial, prefectural, civil security crisis unit);

–the implemented contingency plan (SIP, CSP, IOP, etc.);

–the overall complexity level expected from the simulation.

In addition, this simulation training platform is a support medium for research and experimentation on themes related to the development of a semi-virtual environment with multi-agent simulation (Tena-Chollet 2012), the optimized scripting of exercises

(Limousin 2017; Fréalle 2018), the assessment of performances and aid for the construction of debriefing (Lapierre 2016) and the activation of playful resources during simulation for increasing educational impact (Goutx 2017). These multidisciplinary and integrating themes are also promoters of joint research with industrial partners (as, for example, in the nuclear field) and of collaborative projects with public funding (ANR-2014 SPICy; https://www. YouTube.com/watch?v=OcaAg_zaSdk).

What is more, this platform facilitates the implementation of simulations useful for testing new tools or approaches, whether they are technological, organizational or experimental ones.

1.6. Conclusion

The crisis unit is a complex study and research object. Crisis management systems and organizations are clearly identified, and yet, responses structured in this way to face a crisis are not effective enough. Preparation and crisis management training have become essential components, which can help participants to better address emergency situations or critical events.

The optimal preparation for crisis management is complex to learn, especially for trainees who are not crisis professionals (e.g. security or civil defense services), but who may nonetheless have to face a crisis. In order to meet this need, the law requires or encourages actors to carry out exercises. Crisis management training may adopt different aspects and should be adjusted to the knowledge and skills of trainees. Therefore, it appears that crisis management simulation is the best compromise to provide training for crisis management at a rather strategic level.

Social concern and expectations are important for this topic, which are reflected by abundant research, as will be shown in the following chapters.

1.7. References

Ahlstrom, V., Koros, A., and Heiney, M. (2000). *Team Processes in Airway Facilities Operations Control Centers*. National Technical Information Service, Springfield, VA.

Alvarez, J. (2007). Du jeu vidéo au serious game : approches culturelle, pragmatique et formelle. PhD Thesis, Toulouse 2.

Argillos (2004). *Esquisse d'un Alphabet de la Surprise*. Argillos.

Autissier, D., Bensebaa, F., and Boudier, F. (2012). *L'atlas du management*. Eyrolles, Paris.

Banks, J. (2000). Introduction to simulation. *2000 Winter Simulation Conference*, 10–13 December 2000, Orlando, FL, pp. 9–16.

Banks, J. (2001). Panel session: education for simulation practice – five perspectives, *2001 Winter Simulation Conference*, 9–12 December 2001, Arlington, VA.

Bapst, C. and Gaspar, P. (2011). L'Europe de la formation. In *Traité des sciences et des techniques de la Formation*, Carré, P. and Gaspar, P. (eds). Dunod, Paris.

Becerra, S., Perltier, A., Antoine, J. M., Labat, D., Chorda, J., Ribolzi, O., Daupras, F., and Dartus, D. (2013). Comprendre les comportements face à un risque d'inondation modéré. Etude de cas dans le périurbain toulousain (Sud-Ouest de la France). *Hydrol. Sci. J.*, 58(5), 945–965.

Bernard, L. (2014). *Guide pratique de formation par la simulation*. VA Presse, Paris.

Blanchard, B.W. (2008). Guide to emergency management and related terms, definitions, concepts, acronyms, organization, programs, guidance, executive orders and legislation: a tutorial on emergency management, broadly defined, past and present. Lexicon, US Federal Emergency Management Agency (FEMA), Emmitsburg.

Boin, A. (2004). Crisis Simulations: Exploring Tomorrow's Vulnerabilities and Threats. *Simul. Gaming*, 35(3), 378–393. http://doi.org/10.1177/1046878104266220.

Borodzicz, E.P. and Van Haperen, K. (2002). Individual and group learning in crisis simulations. *J. Contingencies Crisis Manag.*, 10(3), 139–147, 2002.

Bouglet, T. (2002). Incertitude et environnement : Essai de représentation et analyse des choix publics. PhD Thesis, University Panthéon-Sorbonne–Paris I and U.F.R Sciences économiques.

Bristow, D., Shepherd, C.D., Humphreys, M., and Ziebell, M. (2011). To Be Or Not To Be: That Isn't the Question! An Empirical Look at Online Versus Traditional Brick-and-Mortar Courses at the University Level. *Marketing Edu. Rev.*, 21(3), 241–250.

Bruinsma, G. and De Hoog, R. (2006). Exploring protocols for multidisciplinary disaster response using adaptive workflow simulation. *3rd International ISCRAM Conference*, 14–17 May, Newark.

Carroll, J.M. (2000). Five reasons for scenario-based design. *Interact. Comput.*, 13(1), 43–60. doi:10.1016/S0953-5438(00)00023-0.

Cesta, A., Cortellessa, G., and De Benedictis, R. (2014). Training for crisis decision making – An approach based on plan adaptation. *Knowl. Based Syst.*, 58, 98–112.

Combalbert, L. and Delbecque, E. (2012). *La gestion de crise*. PUF, Paris.

Cortes Buitrago, G. (1999). Simulations et Contrôle Pédagogique : Architectures Logicielles Réutilisables. PhD Thesis, Joseph Fourier University, Grenoble.

Crampes, M. and Saussac, G. (1998). L'acte d'apprentissage au cœur de la simulation. *Colloque international NTICF (Nouvelles Technologies de l'Information et de la Communication dans les Formations d'Ingénieurs et dans l'Industrie)*, 18–20 November, INSA, Rouen.

Crampes, M. and Saussac, G. (1999). Facteurs de qualité et composantes de scénario pour la conception de simulateurs pédagogiques à vocation comportementale. *Sci. Tech. Édu.*, 6(1), 11–36.

Crichton, M.T. (2001). Training for decision making during emergencies. *Horizons of Psychol.*, 10(4), 7–22.

Crichton, M.T. (2009). Improving team effectiveness using tactical decision games. *Safety Sci.*, 47(3), 330–336.

Crichton, M.T. and Flin, R. (2004). Identifying and training non-technical skills of nuclear emergency response teams. *Ann. Nucl. Energy*, 31(12), 1317–1330. http://doi.org/10.1016/j.anucene.2004.03.011.

Crichton, M.T., Flin, R., and Rattray, W.A.R. (2000). Training Decision Makers – Tactical Decision Games. *J. Contingencies Crisis Manag.*, 8(4), 208–217. http://doi.org/10.1111/1468-5973.00141.

Crocq, L., Huberson, S., and Vraie, B. (2009). *Gérer les grandes crises sanitaires, économiques, politiques et économiques*. Odile Jacob, Paris.

Csikszentmihalyi, M. (1991). *Flow: The Psychology of Optimal Experience*. Harper Perennial, New York.

Dautun, C. (2007). Contribution à l'étude des crises de grande ampleur: connaissance et aide à la décision pour la Sécurité Civile. PhD Thesis, Ecole Nationale Supérieure des Mines de Saint-Etienne.

Dautun, C. and Lacroix, B. (2013). Crise et décision : plongée au coeur des cellules de crise. *Cahiers de La Sécurité*, 24.

Dautun, C., Pardini, G., and Roux-dufort, C. (2011). La formation des acteurs publics à la gestion de crise : Le cas français. *11th Conference on Civil Security*, 16–17 February.

Denis, H. (1993). *Gérer les catastrophes, l'incertitude à apprivoiser*. Les Presse de l'Université de Montréal, Montreal.

Department of Homeland Security FEMA (2005). *Homeland Security Exercise and Evaluation Program, Volume V: Prevention Exercises*. Washington, DC.

Department of Homeland Security FEMA (2013). *Homeland Security Exercise and Evaluation Program*. Washington, DC.

Department of Homeland Security FEMA (2015). *Training Glossary*.

Direction de la Défense et de la Sécurité Civile (2005). *Plan Communal de Sauvegarde : Guide pratique d'élaboration*. Paris.

Edmond, P. (2011). Crise et Improvisation Organisationnelle : les leçons de quatre études de cas. PhD Thesis, University of Strasbourg.

Fréalle, N. (2018). Formation à la gestion de crise à l'échelle communale : méthode d'élaboration et de mise en oeuvre de scénarios de crise crédibles, pédagogiques et interactifs. PhD Thesis, University of St-Etienne.

Gaultier-Gaillard, S., Persin, M., and Vraie, B. (2012). *Gestion de crise - Les exercices de simulation : de l'apprentissage à l'alerte*. Afnor, Paris.

Goebel, D.J. and Humphreys, M.A. (2014). The Relationships Among Student Learning Styles, Course Delivery Method, and Course Outcomes : A quasi-experiment investigating the case method of course delivery. *Atl. Mark. J.*, 3(2), 4.

Goodrich, D.C. and Edwards, F.L. (2014). Improvised explosive devices. In *Crisis and Emergency Management: Theory and Practice*, 2nd edition, Farazmand, A (ed.). CRC Press, Boca Raton.

Goutx, D. (2014). Réaliser la gravité d'enjeux abstraits à travers une simulation : comprendre COP-RW comme un rite de passage. *Négociations*, 2, 17–28. doi:10.3917/neg.022.0017.

Goutx, D. (2017). Ludicité des simulations de crise, ce qui se joue au cœur d'une crise simulée. *Journée de la Recherche*, 16 October, Alès.

Guarnieri, F., Travadel, S., Martin, C., Portelli, A., and Afrouss, A. (2015). *L'accident de Fukushima DaiIchi, Le récit du directeur de la centrale*. Vol. 1, L'anéantissement.

Guarnieri, F., Travadel, S., Martin, C., Portelli, A., Afrouss, A., and Eric, P. (2016). *L'accident de Fukushima Dai Ichi*. Presses des Mines, Paris.

Guéraud, V. (2003). Pour une ingénierie des situations actives d'apprentissage, Environnements interactifs pour l'apprentissage humain. *EIAH 2003 Conference*, Strasbourg, France.

Guéraud, V. (2005). Approche Auteur pour les Situations Actives d'Apprentissage: Scénarios, Suivi et Ingénierie. Thesis, Joseph Fourier University, Grenoble.

Guzzo, R. and Salas, E. (1995). *Team effectiveness and decision making in organizations.* Pfeiffer, San Francisco.

Heiderich, D. (2010). *Plan de gestion de crise : organiser, gérer et communiquer en situation de crise*. Dunod, Paris.

Heinzen, B. (1995). Crisis Management and Scenarios: the Search for an Appropriate Methodology. Ministry of Home Affairs, The Hague.

Helmreich, R.L., Foushee, H.C., Benson, R., and Russini, W. (1986). Cockpit resource management: exploring the attitude-performance linkage. *Aviat. Space Environ. Med.*, 57, 1198–1200.

Henriksen, K., Battles, J., Keyes, M., and Grady, M. (2008). *Advances in patient safety: New directions and alternatives approaches, Vol. 2: Culture and Redesign.* AHRQ Publication No. 08-0034-2. Agency for Healthcare Research and Quality, Rockville, MD.

Hotte, R. (2016). Modélisation d'environnements fonctionnels. *Journée Scientifique du LICEF.* pp. 89–93

Hussain, T., Feurzeig, W., Cannon-Bowers, J., Coleman, S., Koenig, A., Lee, J., Menaker, E., Moffitt, K., Pounds, K., Roberts, B., Seip, J., Souders, V., and Wainess, R. (2010). Development of game-based training systems: lessons learned in an inter-disciplinary field in the making. In *Serious Game Design and Development: Technologies for Training and Learning*, Cannon-Bowers, J. and Bowers, C. (eds), IGI Global, Hershey, 47–80.

Idasiak, V., Pensec, R., Olivier, N. (2006). Virtual POI: Method and tools, *15ème congrès de maîtrise des risques et de sûreté de fonctionnement*, Lille.

Joab, M., Guéraud, V., Auzende, O. (2005). Les Simulations pour la Formation. In *Environnements Informatiques et Apprentissages Humains*, Grandbastien, M. and Labat, J.-M. (eds), Hermès-Lavoisier, Paris.

Kanki, B.G. (2010). Communication and Crew Resource Management. In *Crew Resource Management*, Kanki, B.G., Helmreich, R. and Anca, J. (eds), Academic Press, Cambridge. http://doi.org/10.1016/B978-0-12-374946-8.10004-4.

Kim, D.-Y., Choe, Y., and Kim, S.-A. (2015). Implementing a digital model for smart space design: Practical and pedagogic issues. *Procedia - Soc. Behav. Sci.*, 174, 3306–3313.

Kincaid, J.P., Donovan, J., Pettitt, B. (2003). Simulation techniques for training emergency response. *Int. J. Emerg. Manag.*, 1(3), 238–246.

King, H.B., Battles, J.B., Baker, D.P., Alonso, A., Salas, E., Webster, J., and Grady, M.L. (2008). TeamSTEPPS: Team strategies and tools to enhance performance and patient safety. In *Advances in Patient Safety: New Directions and Alternative Approaches (Vol. 3: Performance and Tools)*, Henriksen, K., Battles, J., Keyes, M. and Grady, M. (eds), Agency for Healthcare Research and Quality, Rockville.

Klein, G. (1997). The recognition-primed decision (RPD) model: looking back, looking forward. In *Naturalistic Decision Making*, Zsambok, C. and Klein, G. (eds), Lawrence Erlbaum Associates, Inc., Hillsdale.

Kontogiannis, T. and Kossiavelou, Z. (1999). Stress and team performance: Principles and challenges for intelligent decision aids. *Safety Sci.*, 33(3), 103–128. http://doi.org/10.1016/S0925-7535(99)00027-2.

Kouabenan, D.R., Cadet, D., and Sastre, M.T.M. (2006). *Psychologie du risque : identifier, évaluer, prévenir*. De Boeck, Brussels.

Kovordanyi, R., Schreiner, R., Jenvald, J., Eriksson, H., and Rankin, A. (2012). Real-time Support for Exercise Managers' Situation Assessment and Decision Making, *ISCRAM12*, April, Vancouver, pp. 1–5, 2012.

Kowalski-Trakofler, K. M., Vaught, C., and Scharf, T. (2003). Judgment and decision making under stress: an overview for emergency managers. *Int. J. Emerg. Manag.*, 1(3), 278. http://doi.org/10.1504/IJEM.2003.003297.

Labat, J.M., Pernin, J.P., Guéraud, V. (2006). Contrôle de l'activité de l'apprenant: suivi, guidage pédagogique et scénarios d'apprentissage. In *Environnements informatiques pour l'apprentissage humain*, Grandbastien, M. and Labat, J.-M. (eds), Hermes-Science Lavoisier, Paris.

Lachtar, D. (2012). Contribution des systèmes multi-agent à l'analyse de la performance organisationnelle d'une cellule de crise communale. PhD Thesis, Ecole Nationale Supérieure des Mines de Paris, Paris.

Lagadec, P. (1995), *Cellule de crise, les conditions d'une conduite efficace*. Les éditions d'Organisation, Paris.

Lagadec, P. (2010). La Force de Réflexion Rapide – Aide au pilotage des crises. Préventique Sécurité, 112 pp. 31–35, 2010.

Lagadec, P. (2012). *Du risque majeur aux mégachocs*. Préventique, Bordeaux.

Lagadec, P. (2015). *Le continent des imprévus - Journal de bord des temps chaotiques*. Ed. Manitoba/Les Belles Lettres. Paris.

Lagadec, P. and Guilhou, X. (2002a). *La fin du risque zéro*. Eyrolles, Paris.

Lagadec, P. and Guilhou, X. (2002b). Les conditions de survenue des crises graves. In *Conditions et mécanismes de production des défaillances, accidents et crises*, Amalberti, R., Fuchs, C. and Gilbert, C. (eds), Publications de la MSH-ALPES, Grenoble, pp. 157–210.

Lapierre, D., (2016). Méthode EVADE : Une approche intégrée pour l'EValuation et l'Aide au DEbriefing. PhD Thesis, Université de Nîmes-IMT Mines Alès.

Lee, D.A., Ford, N.P., Freeland, R.L., Hough, J.A., Bridge, G.G. (2006). Guidelines for Transportation Emergency Training Exercises. McCormick Taylor Firm.

Lhuillier, B. (2011). *Concevoir un seriousgame pour un dispositif de formation*. FYP Editions, Paris.

Limousin, P. (2017). Contribution à la scénarisation pédagogique d'exercices de crise, PhD Thesis, Ecole Nationale Supérieure des Mines de Saint-Etienne.

Llory, M. (1996). *Accidents industriels : le coût du silence. Opérateurs privés de parole et cadres introuvables*. L'Harmattan, Paris.

Lourdeaux, D. (2001). Réalité Virtuelle et Formation: Conception d'Environnements Virtuels Pédagogiques, PhD Thesis, Ecole des Mines de Paris, Paris.

Lukosch, H., van Ruijven, T., Verbraeck, A. (2012). The participatory design of a simulation training game. *Proceedings of the 2012 Winter Simulation Conference (WSC)*, pp. 1–11. doi:10.1109/WSC.2012.6465218.

MAEE (2017). La diplomatie de l'Urgence, Centre de crise, Ministère des Affaires étrangères et du Développement international. Available: https://www.diplomatie.gouv.fr/IMG/pdf/cdcs_2017-web_cle8b741e-1.pdf

Maisonneuve, D. (2010). *Les relations publiques dans une société en mouvance*, 4th edition. PUQ, Sainte-Foy.

Marks, M.A., Mathieu, J.E. and Zaccaro, S.J. (2001). A temporally based framework and taxonomy of team processes. *Acad. Manag. Rev.*, 26(3), 356–376. http://doi.org/10.5465/AMR.2001.4845785.

Martin, G. (2014). La place des communautés d'utilisateurs dans les dispositifs de gestion de crise. *Les médias sociaux en gestion d'urgence (M.S.GU.)*, ENSOSP.

Mellet d'Huart, D. (2001). La réalité virtuelle: un média pour apprendre, *Cinquième Coloque Hypermédias et Apprentissage*, Grenoble, France.

Mendonca, D., Beroggi, G.E.G., Gent, D. and Wallace, W.A. (2006). Designing gaming simulations for the assessment of group decision support systems in emergency response. *Safety Sci.*, 44(6), 523.

Morin, M., Jenvald, J., Thorstensson, M. (2004). Training first responders for public safety using modeling, simulation, and visualization, SIMSafe, Karlskoga.

Moulin, M.-C. (2014). *La gestion des crises "hors cadre", "L'inconcevable n'est pas impensable !"*. L'Harmattan, Paris.

Nissen, E. (2009). Formation hybride vs. présentielle en langues : effets sur la perception des apprenants liés au mode de formation et à l'encadrement pédagogique. Recherches en didactique des langues et des cultures. *Les Cahiers de l'Acedle*, 6 (6–1), 197–220.

Noori, N.S., Wang, Y., Comes, T. (2017). Behind the Scenes of Scenario-Based Training : Understanding Scenario Design and Requirements in High-Risk and Uncertain Environments. *Proceedings of the 14th ISRAM Conference*, Albi, France.

O'Connor, P. (2007). Naval Aviation Schools Command Pensacola, FL.

O'Connor, P. and O'Dea, A. (2002). The U.S. Navy's aviation safety program: A critical review. *Int. J Appl. Aviation Stud.*, 7(2): 312–328.

Orasanu, J.M. (2010). Flight crew decision-making. In *Crew Resource Management*, Kanki, B., Helmreich, R. and Anca, J. (eds), Academic Press, Cambridge. http://doi.org/10.1016/B978-0-12-374946-8.10005-6

Pastré, P. (2005). Apprendre par la résolution de problèmes: le rôle de la simulation. In *Apprendre par la simulation - De l'analyse du travail aux apprentissages professionnels*, Pastré, P. (ed.), Toulouse, France, 2005.

Pastré, P., Vergnaud, G. (2011). *L'ingénierie didactique professionnelle*. In *Traité des sciences et des techniques de la Formation*, Carré, P. and Gaspar, P. (eds), Dunod, Paris.

Pearson, C.M., Kovoor-Misra, S., Clair, I.I., Mitroff, J.A. (1997). Managing the Unthinkable. *Organizational Dynamics*, 26(2), 51–64.

Pernin, J.-P. (1996). M.A.R.S. Un modèle opérationnel de conception de simulations pédagogiques, PhD Thesis, Université Joseph Fourier - Grenoble I, Grenoble.

Power, D., Henn, P., Power, T., and McAdoo, J. (2013). An evaluation of high fidelity simulation training for paramedics in Ireland. *Int. Paramed. Pract.*, 2(1), 11–18.

Quarantelli, E.L. (1988). Disaster crisis management: a summary of research findings. *J. Manag. Stud.*, 25(4), 373–385. http://doi.org/DOI: 10.1111/j.1467-6486.1988.tb00043.x.

Querrec, R. (2002). Les systèmes multi-agents pour les environnements virtuels de formation, PhD Thesis, Université de Bretagne Occidentale.

Quinton, A. (2007). Besoins, finalités, programmes, objectifs opérationnel.

Rehmann, A. (1995). A Handbook of Flight Simulation Fidelity Requirements for Human Factors Research, Federal Aviation Administration Centre.

Renaudin, H. and Altemaire, A. (2007). *Gestion de crise mode d'emploi, Principes et outils pour s'organiser et manager les crises.* Editions Liaisons, Paris.

Renger, R., Wakelee, J., Bradshaw, J., and Hites, L. (2009). Steps in writing an effective master scenario events list. *J. Emerg. Manag.*, 7(6), 51–60.

Rohrer, M.W. (2000). Seeing in believing: the importance of visualization in manufacturing simulation. *The 2000 Winter Simulation Conference*, 10–13 December 2000, Orlando, FL, pp. 1211–1216.

Roux-Dufort, C. and Ramboatiana, S. (2006). Gestion de crise : les managers possédés par leurs démons. *Magazine de la communication de crise et sensible*, Observatoire International des Crises.

Salas, E. and Cannon-Bowers, J.A. (2001). The science of training : A decade of progress. *Ann. Rev. Psychol.*, 52(1), 471–499.

Salas, E., Dickinson, T.L., Converse, S.A., and Tannenbaum, S.I. (1992). Toward an understanding of team performance and training. In *Teams: their training and performance*, Swezey, R.W. and Salas, E. (eds). Norwood, pp. 3–29.

Sauvagnargues, S., Poppi, J.-C. (2012). Cartographies opérationnelles. In *Incendies de forêts : défis et perspectives*, Sauvagnargues, S. (ed.). Hermes-Lavoisier, pp. 265–302.

Sayegh, L., Anthony, W.P., and Perrewé, P.L. (2004). Managerial decision-making under crisis: The role of emotion in an intuitive decision process. *Hum. Resour. Manag. Rev.*, 14(2), 179–199. http://doi.org/ 10.1016/j.hrmr.2004.05.002

Schank, R.C. (1992). Goal-Based Scenarios, Technical Report no. 36, pp. 61–21.

Schurr, N., Patil, P., Pighin, F., Tambe, M. (2006). Using multiagent teams to improve the training of incident commanders. In *5th International Joint Conference on Autonomous Agents and Multi Agent Systems (AAMAS) Industry Track*, ACM, New York, NY.

Seppänen, H., Mäkelä, J., Luokkala, P., and Virrantaus, K. (2013). Developing shared situational awareness for emergency management. *Safety Sci.*, 55, 1–9. http://doi.org/10.1016/j.ssci.2012.12.009.

Shanahan, C., Best, C., Finch, M., and Sutton, C. (2007). Measurement of the behavioural, cognitive, and motivational factors underlying team performance. Report, Australian Department of Defence, Defence Science and Technology Organisation (DSTO).

Shapiro, M.J., Gardner, R., Godwin, S.A., Jay, G.D., Lindquist, D.G., Salisbury, M.L., and Salas, E. (2008). Defining team performance for simulation-based training: Methodology, metrics, and opportunities for emergency medicine. *Acad. Emerg. Med.*, 15(11), 1088–1097. http://doi.org/10.1111/j.1553-2712.2008.00251.x.

Shrivastava, P., Mitroff, I., and Alpaslan, C.M. (2012). Imagining an education in crisis management. *J. Manag. Edu.*, 37(1), 6–20. doi:10.1177/1052562912455418.

Smith, W. and Dowell, J. (2000). A case study of co-ordinative decision making in disaster management. *Ergonomics*, 48(8), 1153–1166.

Solucom Management & IT Consulting (2014). QSE : qualité et gouvernance des systèmes d'information Module n°4 : la gestion de crise. INSA Toulouse, 2014. [Online]. Available: http://moodle.insa-toulouse.fr/pluginfile.php/44681/mod_resource/content/1/QSE 2014 - Solucom - 4. La gestion de crise 1.0.pdf.

Stern, E.K. (2014). *Designing Crisis Management Training and Exercises for Strategic Leaders*. Försvarshögskolan, Stockholm.

Suchet, R. (2015), La gestion du nucléaire en crise - Une étude à travers les représentations des gestionnaires de crise. PhD Thesis, University of Montpellier 1.

Sundstrom, E., de Meuse, K.P., and Futrell, D. (1990). Work teams: Applications and effectiveness. *Am. Psychol.*, 45(2), 120–133. http://doi.org/10.1037/0003-066X.45.2.120.

Tena-Chollet, F. (2012). Elaboration d'un environnement semi-virtuel de formation à la gestion stratégique de crise, basé sur la simulation multi-agents. PhD Thesis, École Nationale Supérieure des Mines de Saint-Etienne.

Tissington, P. and Flin, R. (2005). Assessing risk in dynamic situations: lessons from fire service operations. *Risk Manag.*, 7(4), 43–51.

Van Vliet, A.J. and Van Amelsfoort, D. (2008). *Multinational military teams.* Multinational Military Operations and Intercultural Factors, NATO OTAN.

Vaughan, A. (1996). *The Challenger Launch Decision: Risky Technology, Culture, and Deviance at NASA (University).* Chicago and London.

Vraie, B., Huberson, S., and Crocq, L. (2010). Cellule de crise et dynamique de groupe. *Magazine de La Communication de Crise et Sensible,* 4–9.

Weick, K.E. (1995). *Sensemaking in Organizations.* Sage, Thousand Oaks.

Weil, S.A., Hussain, T.S., Diedrich, F.J., Ferguson, W. and MacMillan, J. (2004). Assessing distributed team performance in DARWARS training: Challenges and methods. *Proceedings of the Interservice/Industry Training, Simulation, and Education Conference,* Orlando, FL, 2004.

Wybo, J.L. (2009). Le retour d'expérience. Un processus d'acquisition de connaissances et d'apprentissage. In *La Gestion de crise: le maillon humain au sein de l'organisation,* Specht, M. and Planchette, G. (eds). Economica, Paris.

2

Towards A Serious Game Within the Frame of Major Crisis Simulations for Decision-makers: How Do We Connect the DOTs?

2.1. Introduction

Serious games and simulation-based learning exercises are useful training approaches in crisis management. When major crises occur, organizations face critical concerns, such as stress, uncertainties, and the need for quick anticipation and better communication in order to mitigate consequences or avoid negative impacts on high-stake elements. Many factors are critical in a training environment to ensure that effective learning occurs, mainly experience improvement, engagement and immersion, and realism. In a previous piece of work, a set of recommendations was proposed to specify the main components of an improved training environment (Tena-Chollet et al. 2016b). More specifically, we proposed to consider 10 DOTs (Degrees of Training). These DOTs are structured in general, intermediate and specific skills that must be involved in each crisis scenario. In this chapter, we show how to connect the DOTs. To do so, we transpose our previous specifications to the technical requirements of a real semi-virtual training environment (SVTE),

Chapter written by Florian TENA-CHOLLET, Aurélia BONY-DANDRIEUX, and Jérôme TIXIER.

which is presented here. We also demonstrate the advantages of two developed software programs: a dynamic crisis simulation kernel based on a multi-agent system (called "Asymut" for Agent and SYnopsys Management UTility) and a crisis scenario manager (called "SimulCrise").

In the field of major risks, a crisis is characterized by a loss of control and thus a high level of stress for the stakeholders involved due to a "spark event" (i.e. an unexpected trigger) causing a disruption of the balance of a system (e.g. an organization, an infrastructure, a territory). When major crises occur, stakeholders are organized through a crisis unit. The human factor, the management of resources or the uncertainty of the situation are often major sources of vulnerability in the decision-making process of a crisis unit (Smith and Dowell 2000; Morin *et al.* 2004). Conversely, decision-making, communication, mental model sharing, leadership and coordination are useful skills (Lagadec 2012). Theoretically, the processes of decision-making can be creative, analytical, procedural or naturalistic. In practice, a crisis involves critical stakes, significant effects and limited reaction times, and the decision-making process is thus mainly naturalistic (Tena-Chollet 2012). This raises the following paradox: while crises are exceptional, decision-making during crisis often depends on previously experienced situations.

We can note that most training environments for crisis management present shortcomings or limits. They are intended for tactical or operational levels (emergency services, firemen, etc.), and not for strategic ones (stakeholders, for example). The study of other existing environments using functional exercises in crisis management has identified several limits (Tena-Chollet *et al.* 2016b). It is possible to distinguish those related to the unsuitability of the teaching strategy for the profile of learners and those relating to the complexity of moderation for trainers.

On the one hand, it is necessary to facilitate a proactive and participating immersion of learners in a realistic environment and in a group that is as homogeneous as possible in terms of knowledge and experience. On the other hand, the role of trainers is difficult as their authority may not be granted in a group of experts in crisis management. Nevertheless, they must promote success and explain the failures with factual reasons (particularly during the debriefing), while maintaining a certain distance from learners. Some of these difficulties seem to be solved by the use of computer-assisted training (Kebritchi and Hirumi 2008). Training in crisis management through crisis simulation aims to facilitate the transposition of learned skills from theory to practice: learners can share their experiences, knowledge and points of view in order to experience new ways of thinking.

Our research studies how to create an immersive environment for learners who have different profiles of experience, and how to simulate pedagogical crisis scenarios in a playful and realistic manner. Recent works demonstrate that simulation games, like serious games, are effective tools in the teaching of management techniques and engineering, and have been widely used in experiential learning (Mawdesley *et al.* 2011). We have therefore chosen to target the following three domains of improvements (Tena-Chollet *et al.* 2016b):

– the teaching strategy, in order to help trainers to create educational scenarios, to observe learners and to prepare the debriefing phase;

– the simulation system, which must help to make real-time, slow-time or fast-time simulations in order to simplify or highlight the studied phenomena and to immerse learners in a credible scenario;

– the training environment, with the aim of deploying immersion devices and simulation kernels.

Then, we present our methodology, and more specifically:

– the definition of "Degrees of Training" (the DOTs);

– the way to connect the DOTs, with a definition of the required skills in crisis management;

– the activation of the skills by a crisis scenario;

– the scenario execution through a semi-virtual training environment (SVTE);

– the first elements of serious gaming in a real infrastructure for crisis management training.

2.2. State of the art

2.2.1. *Teaching strategy*

Learning processes are part of the "perception-data-information-knowledge-wisdom-vision" cycle, ensuring that decision-making does not affect the environment in which the group is situated (Le Bas 1993; Guéraud 2005; Tena-Chollet 2012). The sequence of these steps entails two prerequisites. The first is that any educational event must be perceptible in order to be picked up by the learner. The second highlights the need to integrate the heterogeneity of learner profiles in the same group. Four classical approaches, namely behaviorism, cognitivism, constructivism and social constructivism, differ in this respect (Werhane *et al.* 2011; Ertmer and Newby 2013).

Social constructivism deals with the problems of collective learning better, but does not focus on the definition of a pedagogical framework suited to the learner profiles (Morin *et al.* 2004; Guéraud 2005). We therefore propose to extend the social constructivist approach through a continuum of organizational learning that is structured around three steps, depending on whether the group is neophyte, intermediate or expert in crisis management. We will call these three steps the "beginner mode", "intermediate mode" and "expert mode". In line with Pasin and Giroux, our approach highlights the need to develop specific educational objectives and different assessment levels of learners (Pasin and Giroux 2011). Finally, the learning speed may be higher during the first two modes (Tena-Chollet 2012). An uninitiated audience increases its skills faster than a group of experts. Although our initial topic of research comes from the need to train stakeholders (i.e. experts in crisis management), we also chose to retain the other two learner profiles (neophyte and intermediate people), which are of considerable teaching interest.

2.2.2. *Simulation strategy*

Business intelligence (BI) facilitates the anticipation and understanding of a situation and decision-making. Interactive environments have several advantages: motivating the user, they help him/her to better understand complex or dangerous situations, studying them with a different scale of view (Joab *et al.* 2005; Mendonça *et al.* 2006; Crichton 2009).

The study of the typology of interactive environments for human learning distinguishes simulation games, microworlds and role-playing games. Simulation games are considered suitable for training decision-makers because they integrate models, scenarios, unexpected events, timed processes, roles, procedures, decisions, consequences, indicators, symbols and helpful hardware (Crichton 2009). This type of serious game may consist of simulators for educational purposes, for the acquisition of technical and non-technical skills, of automatic reflexes and of ways of thinking (Connolly *et al.* 2012). These are used for demonstration purposes, self-training, self-assessment or collaborative work. In every case, it relates to a way of learning through discovery and action (Joab *et al.* 2005; Labat *et al.* 2006).

Three modes determine what the dominance of the simulation will be: the position of independence, the position of competition and the position of cooperation (Tena-Chollet 2012). More importantly, the third one has the advantage that learners work together in order to develop their ability to achieve consensual decision-making. It is possible to make real-time, slow-time or fast-time simulations in order to simplify or highlight the studied phenomena but these settings must be justified from a pedagogical point of view (Joab *et al.* 2005). The propensity of people to attach great importance to the visual aspect should encourage developers to allow the use of maps, data, and 2D or 3D representations in order to assess the impact of the crisis unit's planning during the exercise (Morin *et al.* 2004).

2.2.3. *Training environment*

Typically, virtual environments are destined for either technological or educational uses (Mellet D'Huart 2001; Burkhardt 2003). From a pedagogical perspective, they are used to generate didactic interactions and as a form of exercise management (Burkhardt 2003). In practice, the stress of crisis management can be recreated, and so this can lead learners to carry out tasks under conditions close to reality (Lourdeaux 2001). This approach improves the following types of learning: being, knowledge, know-how and social skills.

These objectives can be better achieved through multimedia interfaces, time constraints, information overload (Critical Thinking Training) and visual representations (Sniezek *et al.* 2001; Kebritchi and Hirumi 2008). The use of real data in interaction with a geographical information system is also a good way to ensure the realism of simulations. Several techniques already exist to facilitate integrations into various environments. Nevertheless, the use of virtual representations to produce new information questions its consequences in an environment which aims to reproduce the real conditions of a crisis management situation. For Buche, virtual representations are defined by three elements: immersion, imagination and interaction (Buche *et al.* 2007). We should note that all the three elements theoretically fit the immersive dimension needed in a crisis simulator, the participating and proactive behaviors expected from learners in a serious game.

Two methods of representation are distinguished: virtual reality and virtual simulation (Pernin 1996). A comparison of these two methods highlighted that virtual simulation is more suited to our approach (Tena-Chollet 2012). Like virtual reality, the use of virtual simulations also makes it possible to replay educational sequences, record data of the exercise or take a break. However, virtual simulations allow for greater reversibility actions (Burkhardt 2003), thus giving the environment a strong didactic aspect. Through any user involvement, the virtual simulation makes it possible to repeat a scenario as many times as necessary, to intervene on the kinetics of the event, the occurrence of particular events, adding constraints, resources or concerning the evolution of the scenario. Therefore, the disconnection from existing reality (implied with virtual reality) allows the learner's decisions to be better taken into account, using temporal distortions if necessary, and replaying all the sequences to give the opportunity for retroactive corrections in cases bad choices were made.

The main disadvantage of the virtual simulation comes from the need to constantly feed it with calculated data, simulation models, computational behaviors and more particularly a dynamic generation of crisis scenarios. Flexibility is usually viewed as an important factor in learning environments (Sun *et al.* 2008). We propose using intelligent agents as the modeling paradigm for the crisis simulation.

2.3. Methodology

Our methodology aims to define the concept of "Degrees of Training" (DOT) for the main human factors involved in crisis management and then to connect them with other parts of a training system.

2.3.1. *Definition of "Degrees of Training"*

The expected reactions of learners seem to be spelled out before the training exercise. We propose that the learning strategy and the content of each exercise depend on the profiles of the learners. For example, a raw novice must learn to identify viable strategies based on the crisis phases, while an expert, by contrast, needs to work on interpersonal relationships within the crisis unit. Three teaching strategies will be established. These are associated with various objectives, are all assessed differently, and take into account the type of learner (neophyte, intermediate or expert).

Stress, resources and time management are the three main constraints that can hinder the process of decision-making. Assuming that a crisis imputable to human causes is more difficult to manage due to emotional involvement, the determination of a scenario should therefore both integrate the identified learning objectives and contribute to a motivating context for the crisis unit. More accurately, the instinct of cooperation within a group is activated and strengthened when problems or common difficulties are clearly seen and if there is at least one solution identified by a significant number of members of the group. So, we propose that no event should be induced that cannot be associated with a possible solution. We also note that the cohesion of a training crisis unit must be maintained by a set of events (either recurrent or triggered on demand).

At the same time, learners do not need to know each other or to have previously cooperated in order to be placed in a learning situation. However, automatic reflexes are only learned and reproduced if the context is the same as that for which the exercise is being conducted. It is important to reproduce the environment in which a learner will be during a real crisis. Four positive factors must be taken into account (instinct, learning, intelligence and adaptability) and six psychosocial weaknesses identified (alterability, subjectivity, ignorance, credulity, disaffection or asociality) (Tena-Chollet 2012). We propose to consider these 10 elements as "Degrees of Training" (DOT) in order to define each crisis scenario and lead to an instructive debriefing. Now, the question is: how to connect the DOTs?

2.3.2. *Connecting the DOTs with a definition of the skills required*

Usually, the skills necessary for emergency management through the decision-makers' experience are not clearly specified, nor factually assessed, and thus, the debriefing step is poor (Lagadec 2012).

Through the prism of our DOTs, it is possible to characterize general goals in terms of skills needed (Tena-Chollet 2012).

In order to achieve a common goal, each member of a crisis unit must perform tasks involving teamwork and must mobilize the following non-specific technical skills: anticipation, communication, teamwork, stress management, decision-making and leadership (Rasmussen 1983; Endsley 2001; Crichton 2009). Decisions cannot be taken in full knowledge, but they require the cooperation of emergency management actors who are not always accustomed to working together (Smith and Dowell 2000). These difficulties can lead to a lack of shared mental models between actors and a lack of internal/external communications of the crisis unit.

Therefore, we consider that general, intermediate and specific skills must be specified. We propose six general skills: (1) anticipation, (2) communication, (3) cooperation, (4) stress management, (5) decision-making and (6) strategic steering. These skills are used to achieve five intermediate sets of tasks: (1) management of the crisis consequences, (2) tactical and operational response, (3) crisis unit management, (4) crisis communication and (5) overall view in the short, medium and long terms. In addition, we have identified 16 groups of "expected actions": (1) human management, (2) resource management, (3) hazard assessment, (4) identification of issues involved, (5) strategies for returning to the normal state, (6) protection of threatened high-stake elements, (7) reinforcement management, (8) analysis of the situation, (9) management and (10) arbitration of strategic options, four types of communication – (11) within the crisis unit, with (12) media, (13) authorities or (14) the public, (15) monitoring and forecasting and (16) identifying the possible scenario changes. These 16 skills have to be improved through events and interactions induced by the crisis scenario (Tena-Chollet 2012).

Conventionally, the main phases of a training session are planning, preparation, the exercise itself and debriefing. This last step is very important because it leads to the acquisition of knowledge by a reflexive analysis of the decision-making. The debriefing must follow specific rules. Indeed, the errors made by learners should not lead to a value judgment. The aim of this step is to reveal the origin of these errors and to understand why they occurred (cognitive process of reconstruction). Therefore, we propose the following evaluation categories for all phases of the continuum of organizational learning: anticipation, communication, teamwork, stress management, decision-making and leadership. These elements are thus identified as the main objectives which should be specified. These objectives can be completed in real time by observers with checklists in order to identify how the group organizes itself to deal with the crisis, the leadership involved, the sharing of information, coordination and the way decisions are made. The checklists can give the results of the training room observations to inform facilitators about the trainees' reactions during the exercise.

When a situation begins with incomplete information, and moves forward in time, new information is known and may show that the initial decisions are no longer adequate. Other methods can therefore be investigated in order to identify the profile of the group (from a teamwork point of view) and to focus on the recognition and the management of these potential errors.

Finally, the use of DOTs implies the intervention of one or more trainers. They are essential as they guide learners to the predefined didactic situations. Role-play guides should thus be created in order to help trainers. Nevertheless, it is not recommended that trainers should intervene during an exercise. The way learners will be led to the didactic situations must be defined, insofar as these aspects must be performed implicitly.

2.3.3. *Skills activation by a crisis scenario*

Two main types of scenario can be embedded in a simulator (Tena-Chollet 2012):

– canvas scenarios, setting a number of rules before the beginning and then allowing free interactions to take place;

– programmed scenarios with a set of actions planned in advance; these actions can be optional or not.

We consider that canvas scenarios increase imagination and satisfy all the elements that should be integrated in simulations while enabling the integration of experience feedback.

The 16 skills previously identified have to be activated through events and interactions induced by the crisis scenario. In order to design it, we used a pattern that integrates two approaches: (1) real past crisis scenarios and (2) fictional crisis scenarios. The result includes three steps: expression and analysis of the learning objectives, construction of a set of realistic events, implementation of the crisis scenario created and evaluation of possibilities for managing it. For (1), it is necessary to use a specific framework (e.g. a real past crisis) based on experience feedback analysis about the disaster to be simulated. Then, we reconstitute operational resources deployed and tactical actions performed (simulation parameters). Finally, global events must be identified in order to realistically maintain the future scenario. For (2), we recommend creating a global context, including the definition of strategic, tactical and operational actors possibly involved. Then, it is possible to model the overall system, its subsystems and interactions between each of them. Finally, an experience feedback study in the current field can lead to the identification of credible events to link with pedagogical objectives. The last step consists of making the scenario animation easy with the help of training and assessment aids, developing needed agents, calibrating the speed simulation and validating with test cases.

2.3.4. Scenario execution through a simulation

In order to dynamically simulate a real or fictitious crisis scenario, the multi-agent approach seems to be appropriated, particularly to model canvas-rules (e.g. physical effects or human behaviors), and then to allow the system to self-organize and schedule all the crisis events. The study of the main MAS indicates the BDI approach, which is based on Stimulus-Organization-Reaction models, as a coherent work perspective in order to simulate agents' behaviors during a virtual crisis (Tena-Chollet 2012).

The model we propose distinguishes between three subsystems in the overall crisis environment: dangerous phenomena (fires, explosions, atmospheric and aquatic dispersion, earthquakes, floods, and tsunamis), sensitive issues (human, infrastructural and environmental) and crisis management responses (tactical/operational resources). Static links between each subsystem can be organized in a tree structure. For modeling dynamics of a crisis scenario, we propose to use an organized and systemic risk analysis method known as MOSAR (Périlhon 2007). MOSAR aims to:

– identify technical and operating failures with system and subsystem definitions;

– characterize interactions between hazard sources, hazard propagation and sensitive targets;

– highlight the undesired events that can be produced by their sequencing.

2.3.5. Simulation execution through a semi-virtual training environment (SVTE)

Our previous research on the technical and organizational requirements has suggested the idea of a distributed multitier architecture for freely sharing the expected features (Tena-Chollet *et al.* 2016a, 2016b). Therefore, seven features of our serious game are identified (Figure 2.1): (1) a simulation kernel based on an MAS (multi-agent system), (2) exercise management under the responsibility of a supervisor, (3) exercise management, thanks to trainers, (4) virtual simulation, databases, (5) data warehouse about experience feedbacks and (6 and 7) the two crisis units. We propose the new concept of semi-virtual training environment (SVTE) for this kind of system. Our SVTE model is said to be semi-virtual because a virtual simulation component is used instead of a virtual reality one.

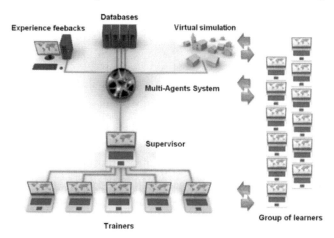

Figure 2.1. *A multitier architecture*

The design of an MAS requires the definition of the global system, expected behaviors of the agents and the agents themselves (Tahir *et al.* 2008). More particularly, the BDI software model (Belief-Desire-Intention) seems to constitute an initial basis in order to simulate human behaviors and accident phenomena (Wooldridge and Jennings 1995). The MAS depends on trainers and their pedagogical objectives as well as the virtual simulation display. This module receives specific input data (physicochemical effects, behavioral models, etc.), which depend on events in a simulated crisis, and involves learner decisions.

The SimulCrise software suite has been developed (in Delphi© language) to support the project in terms of training, pedagogical monitoring and learner assessment. A dedicated multi-agent system named Asymut (Agents and Synopsis Management UTility) has been developed with the help of an existing open source framework called Jade (Java language). The multitier distributed architecture designed during this research led to the identification of seven layers for our SVTE (Figure 2.2).

Figure 2.2. *Components of the multitier distributed architecture*

Except for SEF, all the layers have been developed and integrated into the SimulCrise software suite. ESS is an MAS (Asymut), specially designed and calibrated in order to simulate crisis dynamics. Unlike other approaches which consider the entire training environment as an MAS, Asymut is an SVTE component. This difference stems from the fact that the ESS is considered to be a module used for scenario animation and not as a prerequisite in our engineering system. Learner decisions and trainer guidance are taken into account by the DSA layer. Tracking sheets are used to monitor the scenario events simulated by ESS and to link them to associated learner skills. We should note that these sheets can be preconfigured and/or modified during an exercise in order to integrate new interactions depending on learners' 10 DOTs. However, the main difficulty involved in this process is the association of each new event with a set of skills to be tracked. Finally, centralization in the events log (in the SEF layer) enables tracking sheet enrichment (in the DSA layer).

As shown in Figure 2.3, a summary timeline (1) aims to view the past and upcoming events. New events can also be added and can be linked to a set of agents in Asymut (creation/destruction commands, behavior activation and parameter changes). Georeferenced agents (including archetypical ones) are automatically located on a map (2) in order to help trainers to understand the current state of the crisis simulation. A database of documents is available (4) and aims to send information by email or fax. Indicators (3) and statistics (5) are calculated in real time and feed the debriefing step. Screenshot (6) shows the scenario manager which is an overview of the distributed multitier architecture. The combination of a monitoring tool with Asymut contributes to making the management of complex scenarios easier. Unlike other approaches which consider the entire training environment as a multi-agent system, Asymut is seen as a part of our environment. A software layer including a 3D virtual simulation server helps to immerse learners in a scenario close to reality. Each of these components is associated with man-machine interfaces, providing access to the key features required for a training session exercise (adding major events, setting simulation speed).

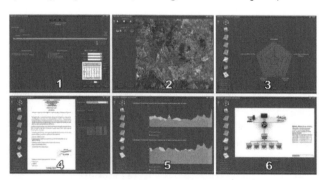

Figure 2.3. *SimulCrise suite – a focus on the scenario manager*

2.3.6. *Towards serious gaming in a real infrastructure for crisis management training*

This research was performed within the framework of a new risk science institute (IMT Mines Alès, France) with the aim of including a crisis management simulator for training decision-makers. Our methodological recommendations have been applied in order to create a physical SVTE (semi-virtual training environment).

Four adjacent rooms have been located so as to carry out two simultaneous exercises (Figure 2.4). The trainers' room allows for the global and non-intrusive supervision of two groups of learners by way of a one-way mirror. Finally, a technical area includes all the elements needed to provide a dynamic training session (software, multimedia hardware and simulation servers).

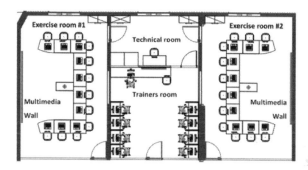

Figure 2.4. *A physical infrastructure design*

The key step in the debriefing led us to consider a particular organizational approach to encourage learners to share the same mental models. To foster both individual and collective reflexive discussion, we propose to have the same crisis scenario managed by two different crisis units at the same time. During the debriefing phase, the sharing of strategies chosen separately by the two groups is intended to foster learning from peers and not from trainers.

As shown in Figure 2.5, five typical layouts of learners are relevant for the training (Noyé and Jacques 2015). (1) The classroom layout fosters a one-way communication and passivity. This slows and fragments the exchange of perceptible information between learners. (2) The meeting room layout helps foster discussion, but the proximity of learners with different skill levels limits the conditions of cooperation. (3) The roundtable layout enables face-to-face contact, but one person is usually the center of attention. (4) The semicircular layout draws attention to a point of interest, while facilitating communication within the group. (5) The working group layout creates "think tanks" without having to move. This layout fosters new ideas for action when there are many learners. The need to facilitate intergroup communication, participation in decision-making and equal access to available information, led us to choose a semicircular layout for learners (fourth layout in Figure 2.5).

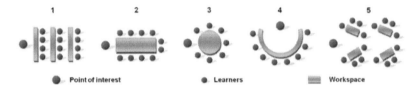

Figure 2.5. *Typical layouts of learners*

Furthermore, five sets of devices are proposed in order to immerse learners in a realistic context. (1) Global immersion devices consist of insulation shutters creating confined rooms in order to remove any external factors (time of day, season, weather), which may interfere with the simulated crisis scenario (we should note that this is usually done in most crisis simulators). (2) Visual immersion devices include a multimedia wall with touch boards. These devices aim to achieve the real-time display of the required information through a customizable and collaborative workspace. (3) Soundscape immersion devices are necessary to transpose some crisis events to perceptible elements (media information, rain, explosion sounds, etc.). (4) Participative immersion devices are intended to reconstruct a crisis unit while guaranteeing the non-intrusive management of trainers. We suggest the use of one-way mirrors between the trainers' room and the two exercise rooms so that trainers can see without being seen. We also propose to deploy monitoring cameras and audio feedback systems in order to more easily follow oral interactions between learners.

(5) Kinesthetic immersion devices mainly include thermal management equipment in learners' rooms. The purpose is to degrade crisis management conditions (heating or air-conditioning failures) and to simulate a context that corresponds to each scenario. It is worth noting that part of these devices must be anticipated before the construction of a new training environment. Finally, learners must interact with trainers, thanks to communication devices commonly used during real crisis management (phones, fax and email).

This crisis simulator can be therefore used as a training platform and as an experimental framework for calibrating, testing and validating new approaches and tools.

2.4. Discussion

We have proposed a methodology of design which implements **seven steps** in order to model a semi-virtual training environment (SVTE) connecting DOTs in the field of crisis management (Figure 2.6). **Step 1** concerns the specification of the environment and integrates the training chronology, the structuration of the subsystems involved and the expected features (what are the immersion devices and software involved? How many people are required for the training session? etc.). Then, a physical infrastructure and information technology architecture can be defined. **Step 2** includes the specification of the users (learners and trainers) and the modalities of interactions (phones? emails? fax? etc.). **Step 3** concerns the kernel design (in the form of a hierarchy of dangerous phenomena), high-stake elements (typology of possible human, material and environmental issues), and tactical and operational actors that have to also be simulated. **Steps 4** and **5** concern the creation and the simulation of a crisis scenario. These steps integrate the educational objectives and imply the specification of activation rules for the events of the scenario. **Step 6** involves the design of man-machine interfaces in order to help trainers to moderate the exercises. Finally, **Step 7** assembles all the techniques and tools required for debriefing. We should note that **Step 3** is in the form of a multi-agent system (MAS).

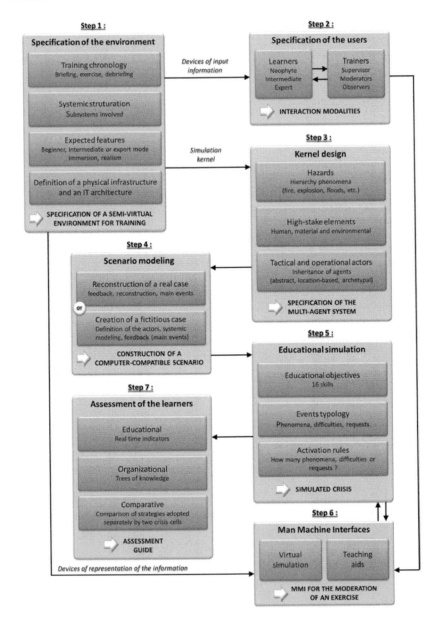

Figure 2.6. *A model proposed for the design*
of a crisis management simulator

The proposed simulator allows our DOTs to connect with any part of this system (learners, expected skills, pedagogical objectives, debriefing step, etc.).

However, there are several limitations of our distributed multitier architecture. The first one comes from the 3D virtual simulation component because the use of this kind of software interface can lead to differences between the planned uses and the results obtained. This constraint stems from the differences between the cognitive models of designers and users, and between learners and trainers.

From a modeling point of view, two main difficulties have been identified using MOSAR. The first one concerns the display of all possible changes in the simulation, which are difficult to interpret because of a large number of events linking all the subsystems of a crisis scenario. This method takes into account all the scenario paths from the point of view of hazard, and it would be interesting to take sequences of actions into account more. Providing the scenario with such a design will give the possibility to imagine all the possible contingencies and to have scripts to make an interactive drama (Si *et al.* 2005). The second difficulty is due to the physical impossibility of providing both an overview of all subsystems (to anticipate next events) and a local view (to provide clear and precise readability). We should note that MOSAR fully performs the functions of modeling a system to be simulated, but does not seem to be appropriate when different levels of dynamic visualization are simultaneously required. It may be interesting to simulate interaction with potential users and keep the story paths for well-motivated users (Si *et al.* 2005). This kind of tool should reduce the design work of a crisis scenario and make the system more efficient.

From the point of view of the scenario designer, it would be easier to design a scenario if data about stakes, hazard, human and material means and emergency organization were available and organized in databases, for instance. Such data management could make it simpler to enter harmonized data into the system. It would be necessary to determine which input data is needed and how it has to be supplied to the system.

2.5. Conclusion

In a crisis unit, decision-makers have to mobilize various technical and non-technical skills through teamwork. However, we have highlighted that the need for experience implies regular training of the stakeholders involved. Our research is situated at the confluence of the pedagogical and technological difficulties typically encountered. The use of functional training exercises may reinforce the importance of the decision-making within a closed group. The basis of this event-based approach to training is the simulation of events that can occur in order to make learners aware of the key concepts at stake. During a virtual exercise, learners must be faced with dilemmas requiring naturalistic decision-making and thus be able to more easily share existing or new mental models. We also recommend integrating the emergency dimension by using a critical-thinking training approach. This makes it possible to raise learners' awareness of optimizing the ratio of reaction time versus the amount of available information.

A typology of educational objectives was identified, with six general skills, five intermediate sets of tasks, and 16 groups of expected actions. All these expected forms of behavior fit our concept of DOTs (Degrees of Training) and must be connected and stimulated by events in a crisis scenario.

We have proposed a new approach to emergency management training and suggest a set of specifications in order to design a semi-virtual environment. Serious games need to define models, scenarios, unexpected events, timed processes, role guides, procedures, decisions, consequences, indicators, symbols and a specific infrastructure. Therefore, our simulator does not actually fully fit the concept of a serious game because formal criteria of the expected playful characteristics are not yet defined. These criteria constitute the main means of improvement in our methodological approach.

From educational and technical points of view, scenarios linked with virtual simulations seem to be a good way to simulate and represent a real or fictitious situation. This approach entails a simulation kernel for which we suggest a multi-agent system. Our methodological recommendations have been applied in order to define a real semi-virtual training environment which integrates five immersion devices, two layouts of learners, a software suite named SimulCrise, a 3D virtual simulation server and a dedicated multi-agent system named Asymut. Since 2011, our experimental approach has been validated by several training exercises with institutional stakeholders, industrialists and students.

Finally, we should note that a specific debriefing methodology is needed to assess learners in order to take into account the 10 DOTs (Degrees of Training) chosen, the performance of the crisis units, the profiles of learners and the skills involved during each exercise. These points will be developed, described and analyzed in our semi-virtual training environment for crisis management.

2.6. References

Buche, C., Querrec, R., De Loor, P., and Chevaillier, P. (2007). MASCARET: A pedagogical multi-agent system for virtual environment for training. In *Online and Distance Learning: Concepts, Methodologies, Tools and Applications 2*, IGI Global, pp. 1137–1156.

Burkhardt, J.-M. (2003). Réalité virtuelle et ergonomie : quelques apports réciproques. *Trav. Hum.*, 66(1), 65–91. doi:10.3917/th.661.0065.

Connolly, T.M., Boyle, E.A., MacArthur, E., Hainey, T., and Boyle, J.M. (2012). A systematic literature review of empirical evidence on computer games and serious games. *Comput. Educ.*, 59, 661–686. doi:https://doi.org/10.1016/j.compedu.2012.03.004.

Crichton, M.T. (2009). Improving team effectiveness using tactical decision games. *Saf. Sci.*, 47, 330–336. doi:http://dx.doi.org/10.1016/j.ssci.2008.07.036.

Endsley, M.R. (2001). Designing for situation awareness in complex systems. In *Proceedings of the Second International Workshop on Symbiosis of Humans, Artifacts and Environment*, Kyoto, Japan.

Ertmer, P.A. and Newby, T.J. (2013). Behaviorism, cognitivism, constructivism: Comparing critical features from an instructional design perspective. *Perform. Improv. Q.*, 26, 43–71. doi:10.1002/piq.

Guéraud, V. (2005). Approche auteur pour les Situations Actives d'Apprentissage : Scénarios, Suivi et Ingénierie. HDR Thesis, University of Grenoble.

Joab, M., Gueraud, V., and Auzende, O. (2005). Les Simulations pour la Formation. In *Environnements Informatiques et Apprentissages Humains*, Grandbastien, M. and Macas, L.J. (eds). Hermès-Lavoisier.

Kebritchi, M. and Hirumi, A. (2008). Examining the pedagogical foundations of modern educational computer games. *Comput. Educ.*, 51, 1729–1743. doi:10.1016/j.compedu.2008.05.004.

Labat, J.-M., Pernin, J.-P., and Guéraud, V. (2006). Contrôle de l'activité de l'apprenant: suivi, guidage pédagogique et scénarios d'apprentissage. In *Environnements Informatiques pour l'Apprentissage Humain, Collection IC2*, Grandbastien, M., Labat, J.-M. (eds). Hermès-Lavoisier, 69–96.

Lagadec, P. (2012). *Du risque majeur aux mégachocs*. Préventique, Bordeaux.

Le Bas, C. (1993). La firme et la nature de l'apprentissage. *Economies et Sociétés*, 27(5), 7–23.

Lourdeaux, D. (2001). Réalité virtuelle et formation : conception d'environnements virtuels pédagogiques. PhD Thesis, École Nationale Supérieure des Mines de Paris.

Mawdesley, M., Long, G., Al-jibouri, S., and Scott, D. (2011). The enhancement of simulation based learning exercises through formalised reflection, focus groups and group presentation. *Comput. Educ.*, 56, 44–52. doi:10.1016/j.compedu.2010.05.005.

Mellet D'Huart, D. (2001). La réalité virtuelle: un média pour apprendre. In *Cinquième colloque Hypermédias et apprentissages*, De Vries E., Pernin J.P., Peyrin J.-P. (eds). EPI; INRP, Grenoble, France.

Mendonça, D., Beroggi, G.E.G., van Gent, D., and Wallace, W.A. (2006). Designing gaming simulations for the assessment of group decision support systems in emergency response. *Saf. Sci.*, 44, 523–535. doi:10.1016/j.ssci.2005.12.006

Morin, M., Jenvald, J., Crissey, M.J., and Systemteknik, V. (2004). Using simulation, modeling and visualization to prepare first responders for homeland defense. In *Proceedings of the Second Swedish-American Workshop on Modeling and Simulation, (SAWMAS-2004)*, 32–39. doi:10.1.1.524.7723.

Noyé, D. and Jacques, P. (2015). *Le guide pratique du formateur: concevoir, animer, évaluer une formation*. Eyrolles.

Pasin, F. and Giroux, H. (2011). The impact of a simulation game on operations management education. *Comput. Educ.*, 57, 1240–1254. doi:https://doi.org/10.1016/j.compedu.2010.12.006.

Périlhon, P. (2007). *La gestion des risques – Méthode MADS-MOSAR II : manuel de mise en oeuvre : application aux installations et plus particulièrement aux installations industrielles*. Les Editions Demos, Paris.

Pernin, J.-P. (1996). M.A.R.S. : un modèle opérationnel de conception de simulations pédagogiques. PhD Thesis, Joseph-Fourier University, Grenoble.

Rasmussen, J. (1983). Skills, rules, and knowledge; signals, signs, and symbols, and other distinctions in human performance models. *IEEE Trans. Syst. Man. Cybern.*, SMC-13, 257–266. doi:10.1109/TSMC.1983.6313160.

Si, M., Marsella, S., Pynadath, D.V. (2005). Thespian: Using multi-agent fitting to craft interactive drama. *Proc. of Fourth Intl. Joint Conf. on Autonomous Agents and Multiagent Systems*, ACM, 21–28.

Smith, W. and Dowell, J. (2000). A case study of co-ordinative decision-making in disaster management. *Ergonomics*, 43, 1153–1166. doi:10.1080/00140130050084923.

Sniezek, J.A., Wilkins, D.C., and Wadlington, P.L. (2001). Advanced training for crisis decision making: simulation, critiquing, and immersive interfaces. *Hawaii International Conference on System Sciences*, 3, 3042. doi:10.1109/HICSS.2001.926337.

Sun, P.-C., Tsai, R.J., Finger, G., Chen, Y.-Y., and Yeh, D. (2008). What drives a successful e-Learning? An empirical investigation of the critical factors influencing learner satisfaction. *Comput. Educ.*, 50, 1183–1202. doi:https://doi.org/10.1016/j.compedu.2006.11.007.

Tahir, O., Andonoff, E., Hanachi, C., Sibertin-Blanc, C., Benaben, F., Chapurlat, V., and Lambolais, T. (2008). A collaborative information system architecture for process-based crisis management. In *Knowledge-Based Intelligent Information and Engineering Systems*, Lovrek, I., Howlett, R.J., and Jain, L.C. (eds). Springer, Berlin.

Tena-Chollet, F. (2012). Elaboration d'un environnement semi-virtuel de formation à la gestion stratégique de crise, basé sur la simulation multi-agents. Ecole Nationale Supérieure des Mines de Saint-Etienne.

Tena-Chollet, F., Fréalle, N., Bony-Dandrieux, A., and Tixier J. (2016a). Design of a semi-virtual training environment (serious game) for decision-makers facing up a major crisis. *Chemical Engineering Transactions*, 48, 853–858. doi:10.3303/CET1648143.

Tena-Chollet, F., Tixier, J., Dandrieux, A., and Slangen, P. (2016b). Training decision-makers: Existing strategies for natural and technological crisis management and specifications of an improved simulation-based tool. *Safety Science*, 97, 144–153. doi: http://dx.doi.org/10.1016/j.ssci.2016.03.025.

Werhane, P.H., Hartman, L.P., Moberg, D., Englehardt, E., Pritchard, M., and Parmar, B. (2011). Social constructivism, mental models, and problems of obedience. *J. Bus. Ethics*, 100, 103–118. doi:10.1007/s10551-011-0767-3.

Wooldridge, M. and Jennings, N.R. (1995). Intelligent agents: Theory and practice. *Knowl. Eng. Rev.*, 10, 115–152. doi:10.1017/S0269888900008122.

Improving Crisis Exercises and Managers' Skills through the Development of Scenario Design

In this chapter, we will discuss the ways of improving the scripting phase of an exercise conception in order to improve crisis management training and experiential learning.

Attention should be given to the elaboration of scenarios, which is based on the scenario's central role in implementing, developing and even maintaining skills. More generally, it mainly contributes to the participants' immersion and involvement in the proposed exercise.

Thus, the scenario is both the heart and the skeleton of the exercise. It is therefore necessary to devote research and analysis to the development of the scenario, making it possible to ensure a rigorous and effective construction (ADPSA 2016), in agreement with the learning expectations and objectives of the participants.

3.1. What is a pedagogical scenario for a crisis exercise?

A scenario is a sequence of events that meets the training objectives. It corresponds to the planned sequence of events of the

Chapter written by Philippe Limousin, Aurélia Bony-Dandrieux, Jérôme Tixier and Sophie Sauvagnargues.

exercise. Scriptwriting is the method of developing and organizing the stimuli that will compose the scenario.

The main purpose of an educational scenario is to develop the learners' skills in an optimal way. Thus, a learning situation must be set up and structured so that scriptwriting becomes pedagogical (Villiot-Leclercq 2006).

Regardless of the field using the exercise simulation for training (digital, military, medical, etc.), four main phases of educational scriptwriting are generally highlighted (Driskell and Johnston 1998, pp. 191–217; Department of Energy 2002; O'connor *et al.* 2002; DDSC 2005):

1) to identify training needs, including the review of lessons learnt from past crises and exercises;

2) to select the pedagogical objectives and define the scope and perimeter of the scenario;

3) to select and organize stimuli within the scenario to address the training objectives;

4) to assess and verify the scenario before its development through the execution of the exercise.

The first item should be completed by the identification of pre-existing skills in the group of participants, in particular, skills necessary to the tasks' execution, performed, for example, as part of emergency procedures (technical skills among others) and organizational skills, essential for teamwork required in crisis management.

3.2. Why and for whom the script is crucial?

The scenario is the central element for different actors of the training, namely participants (purpose of the exercise), animators who set the exercise to music and finally observers/evaluators (who are essential to ensure capitalization of skills acquired during the exercise) (El-Kechai 2008).

The expectations of these different parties differ on how and what should constitute and compose the scenario (Figure 3.1).

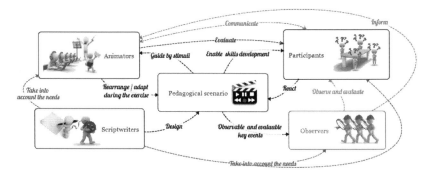

Figure 3.1. *Stakeholders' expectations of the scenario. For a color version of this figure, see www.iste.co.uk/sauvagnargues/crisis.zip*

3.2.1. *Stakes of scriptwriting for participants*

Exercise participants expect a coherent, plausible and credible scenario, but above all, they require that the exercise (and therefore the underlying scenario) enables them to implement or develop their skills (Gaultier-Gaillard *et al.* 2012). Furthermore, the scenario must not be too easy; otherwise, it may allow us to think that crisis management is only based on the easy implementation of procedures and that it will run smoothly.

The scenario must also not be too difficult and rigid (Combalbert 2005). The perverse effect could thus completely demobilize and demotivate the participants facing insurmountable to-do tasks and obstacles. This kind of exercise is completely counterproductive and presents no educational advantage.

3.2.2. *Stakes of scriptwriting for animators*

Concerning animators, the scenario is a guide or framework essential to the development of the exercise. It allows them to inject stimuli at appropriate times during the exercise and to relevant persons.

Moreover, the scenario provides a backdrop to which they can refer in order to react more easily to the participants' answers during the exercise (IRM 2008).

The understanding of the scenario and the implementation by animators are fundamental to ensure the success of the crisis exercise and thus promote participants immersion, their interest in the exercise and therefore their learning.

3.2.3. *Stakes of scriptwriting for observers*

Finally, for observers, two different points of view can be adopted. The first one is based on the total ignorance of the exercise scenario that will be observed. This ensures a very high neutrality in the apprehension of the actions and interactions established between the participants. Conversely, the second considers the scenario as a framework of events, requesting specific reactions and thereby identifying key elements to be observed and evaluated. In this second approach, the scenario construction phase and the creation of observation tools fuel each other (Lapierre 2016).

3.3. How can we improve the pedagogical scripting of crisis exercises?

The implementation of several existing scriptwriting methods (Cohen *et al.* 1998; Fowlkes *et al.* 1998; DSC 2009; Fagel 2014, p. 502; Heiderich and Maroun 2017) has brought to light that they are not directly operational. It has also made it possible to identify several weaknesses and limitations. For example, there is no exhaustive list of training objectives for a crisis exercise.

Moreover, the scriptwriter is not guided in the choice of events to be inserted in the scenario in order to solicit the desired skills or to recreate a crisis universe.

Indeed, the scenarios must be as close as possible to reality in the transcription of a crisis situation, in particular, concerning the inclusion of the stress factor (Gaultier-Gaillard *et al.* 2012).

The lack of crisis characteristic elements in the exercise scenarios (Robert 2002; Combalbert and Delbecque 2012, p. 128; Lagadec 2015; Heiderich and Maroun 2017) justifies the development and improvement of this exercise design stage.

Thus, a scriptwriter faces many difficulties and questions:

– How should a training scenario adapted to the participants be designed? This led us to question (i) the methods for evaluating the level of participants prior to the exercise, (ii) the objectives of scriptwriting, (iii) transforming the pedagogical intentions into stimuli and (iv) the quantity of stimuli to inject into the scenario.

– How can the specific crisis features be replicated in the scenarios? In other words, what stimuli can be used to recreate uncertainty, surprise, etc. and how often should they be inserted into the scenarios in order to reproduce a crisis dynamic?

– How should the scenarios be verified and validated once created, in terms of coherence, difficulty or relevance, particularly concerning the solicitation of learners' skills?

Currently, it is difficult for a scriptwriter to handle all the constraints imposed on crisis exercise scenarios (believable, credible, adapted to the level and skills of the participants, etc.). It is therefore necessary to improve existing methods and tools in order to help the scriptwriter and to contribute to improving crisis management training.

The abovementioned difficulties led us to draw up a list of ways to improve the pedagogical scenario of crisis exercises. Several themes have therefore been identified:

– scripting steps to improve (i) the consideration of participants' characteristics and (ii) the distribution of stimuli in the scenario;

– scriptwriting objectives, in particular, to list pedagogical intentions and define a scenario framework to be respected;

– the links between stimuli and objectives in order to propose to the scriptwriters a method and means to insert learning levers associated with specific skills;

– an evaluation phase of the scenario to contribute to its verification before the development phase.

These four themes have been studied and are addressed in the following sections. It is important to note that our results are based on an iterative process of testing and improvement of the scripting stage since many exercises have been implemented within the simulation facility of IMT Mines Alès or directly within crisis units from administrations or industries.

3.4. Methodology to develop a crisis exercise scenario

The methodology is built on the four main phases of pedagogical scriptwriting. It is necessary to detail them before proposing specific means to make them more operational. First, regardless of the considered step, scriptwriters must always keep in mind for whom, why and how they write.

The scenario created will not necessarily concern all the risks capable of impacting the company or the city. The aim is not to ensure that crisis teams know all conceivable scenarios (which is quite impossible), but that they know how to behave in the face of different situations that may happen. Furthermore, it is necessary to define specific objectives to the participants, their crisis organization and group level.

However, one of the main barriers is the heterogeneity of participants' level within the group, whether this refers to the variable level of knowledge on crisis management of participants, to the individual or collective experience specific to each individual, to the skills and therefore training needs and ultimately to the pedagogical objectives of each person.

Nevertheless, to facilitate scriptwriting, it is possible in a first simplification step to classify the group of participants as either a novice, competent or an expert according to several criteria (experience, knowledge of the territory, etc.).

In addition, scriptwriters must meet specific objectives, particularly in terms of training and reproduction of a crisis situation.

3.4.1. *Prepare the scriptwriting*

Scriptwriting begins by meeting the organization's head of crisis management training and the main stakeholders (participants). The first meeting will enable the scriptwriters to identify and characterize the participants of the exercise and define, with them, the operational and crisis objectives (see section 3.4.2). The duration of the scenario and its perimeter are often defined during this first meeting. Scriptwriters must continue this meeting process during scriptwriting (Borglund and Öberg 2014) in order to mobilize and involve different stakeholders and validate the consistency of the script. By knowing the main events of the scenario, the participating crisis organization can prepare and improve its crisis management before the exercise.

Scriptwriting should not be the prerogative of the scriptwriter alone, since the development of crisis management resources and stakeholder awareness often takes place during this stage. However, it is necessary not to give information to the participants about the scenario (in particular, for an unannounced exercise or for an exercise including a confidential scenario).

Moreover, in many cases, improving the deep understanding of the functioning and the experiences of the crisis organization is an important criterion for the scenario's success.

Finally, it can be relevant for the scriptwriters to establish a mapping of stakeholders from the organization to broaden the scope of the scenario.

3.4.2. *Better define the objectives to achieve*

Scriptwriting starts by identifying key objectives for the exercise (Heiderich 2010).

Thus, three categories of objectives were defined in order to produce a pedagogical scenario dedicated to crisis exercises (Limousin 2017):

Operational objectives (technical or organizational)

They correspond to the expected actions from the participants which will have to be requested by the scenario. For example, an operational objective may be to achieve a situation update, to determine the hazardous phenomenon or to identify threatened issues. These objectives must be identified and selected in a judicious way.

The analysis of several past crises, of various crisis exercises' reviews, of job descriptions and crisis procedures of several crisis team members from different organizations have allowed us to identify nearly 150 operational objectives.

The solicitation of one or several of these objectives by injecting stimuli in the scenario will require that the participants implement specific skills.

When preparing the exercise, it is essential to match these objectives with the function, role, responsibilities, skills (technical and organizational) and needs of participants.

Crisis objectives

This family of objectives aims at offering help to the scriptwriter to reproduce the characteristics of a crisis universe in the scenarios. These objectives correspond in particular to the insertion of ambiguous and uncertain elements, surprise, stress, temporal pressure or wrong tracks (as many elements producing a wide range of emotion and feelings of imminent hazard). Thus, 12 crisis objectives are suggested for the scriptwriting of crisis exercises (Limousin 2017).

Objectives of the pedagogical framework

These objectives represent the creation of a learning situation. In our research work, seven pedagogical framework's objectives have been defined (Limousin 2017): to be coherent and credible, to be relevant, to adapt to the level of the participants, to maintain an appropriate level of involvement, to be a challenge, to keep the participants in suspense and to be immersive.

The definition of these objectives will provide a framework for the scriptwriter in the verification phase and enable him/her to ensure that he/she has met the objectives of the pedagogical scriptwriting for the crisis exercise.

3.4.3. Develop the crisis scene and construct the initial spatio-temporal structure of the scenario

This stage corresponds to the definition phase of the scenario scope, in particular, by identifying the stakes and hazardous phenomena. The scriptwriter may rely on this initial crisis scene for the development of their script and the insertion of learning levers.

Generally speaking, a scenario begins with the occurrence of an important, major event or its announcement (crisis triggering or revealing phenomenon) followed by a sequence of events (Rankin *et al.* 2011, p. 22).

Above all, it is important to identify the number of phenomena and issues adapted to the profile of the participants. We assumed that it was possible to define these quantities on the basis of the analysis of the exercises carried out, observed and evaluated. Consequently, we proposed to inject five to seven phenomena for a three-hour exercise to train experienced learners. This value includes the main phenomena (e.g. floods), precursor phenomena (e.g. runoff), reinforcing phenomena (e.g. wind) or cascading events (e.g. floods) and even independent phenomena.

The value of this parameter is integrated in the calculation of the scenario's difficulty level. Nevertheless, the characteristics of the phenomena and their issues also influence the difficulty index of the scenario. Thus, it is necessary to compare the profile of the participants with the "impact scores" of phenomena and issues (result relative to the evaluation of the impact of the elements on the level of difficulty of the scenario).

Once the number and impact score of phenomena and stakes are in mind, the scriptwriter selects those adapted for the exercise according to (i) the wishes or regulatory obligations of the organization's crisis management training manager, (ii) the profile of the participants, (iii) objectives, (iv) potential animators, (v) the presence or absence of a description of the elements in the contingency plans and (vi) the duration of the scenario. It is then necessary to organize the occurrence of events in the scenario in such a way as to increase the level of difficulty and suspense over time. Once the crisis scene is created, the next step consists of inserting learning levers to solicit all the selected objectives.

3.4.4. *Insert learning levers to solicit training objectives: the obstacles*

The methods for crisis exercises' scriptwriting encourage scriptwriters to insert events related to the selected objectives (Fowlkes *et al.* 1998; FEMA 2017). Nevertheless, it is necessary to define the method for identifying these events and their relationship with the objectives.

The skills of the participants in crisis management must be requested during the exercise through the upstream inclusion of learning levers in the scenario. The CTT method (Cohen *et al.* 1998) uses events that put learners in a degraded situation. In addition, in the artistic field, scriptwriters use conflicts and obstacles to develop their scenario (Lavandier 2014). Thus, based on these methods, we can advise crisis exercise scriptwriters to insert specific obstacles in their scenario to solicit the selected objectives. These obstacles must disrupt the management of the situation and, consequently, ask participants to implement actions associated with the requested objective. Thus, scriptwriters must question the obstacles that would require specific actions to be taken or that would oppose a good execution of situation management. Scriptwriters can use past crises, identified deficiencies of the participating crisis organization and past exercises on the same theme to identify challenges to be included in the scenario.

These considerations led to the creation of a non-exhaustive database of goal-related barrier stimuli (Limousin 2017).

For example:

– if the objective is to test the setting up of a safety perimeter around an accident, then the animators can inform the participants of the presence of many onlookers who may hinder and slower the arrival of emergency services;

– if the objective aims at testing the management of the crisis unit, scriptwriters can insert dilemmas in the scenario. A concrete example is the injection of a message involving the choice between two decisions, implying serious but different losses for each one.

In short, by inserting obstacles, the pedagogical objective is indirectly called and requires participants' initiative. In addition, observation is facilitated because the scriptwriter can propose to the observers to evaluate their capacity to cross an obstacle.

3.4.5. *Insert stimuli to not solicit unselected objectives: support stimuli*

Our research work has led to the definition of "support stimuli". They are designed to help participants when a solicitation asks for the implementation of unselected objectives. Indeed, it proved relevant not to make the participants work on actions that they master and to focus their attention instead on the skills to be tested or improved. Thus, the method (Limousin 2017) suggests injecting support stimuli in the scenario to not work on unselected objectives. To identify the support stimuli of the script, the scriptwriter must find the best way to help participants or to avoid them working on an unselected goal.

3.4.6. *Adjust the number of stimuli to the level and objectives of the participants*

However, the number of obstacles must be limited according to the profile of the participants, in order to maintain their involvement.

The challenge for the scriptwriter includes finding a good compromise in the scenario's difficulty in order to maintain attractiveness to participants of the crisis exercise and to optimize learning (Cook 2006).

As already mentioned, a highly stimulating scenario may frighten and can seriously inhibit participants, creating, for example, discomfort or even strong anxiety, therefore restricting learning. Conversely, an easier scenario can prevent participants' demobilization but if the scenario is too easy, learning becomes poor (FEMA 2017).

It is therefore necessary to adapt the level of difficulty of the scenario to that of the participants.

Thus, we proposed to limit the number of operational objectives to be selected according to the duration of the exercise and the profile of the participants (e.g. between 5 and 10 operational objectives per hour for experienced ones) (Limousin 2017).

Furthermore, the scenario is scalable during the exercise, and animators must have the instinct to adapt in real time, according to the reaction capability of participants, the number of stimuli upward or downward.

3.4.7. *Recreate a crisis universe: crisis stimuli*

"A crisis simulation has as its major goal to recreate a sufficiently uncertain universe" (Heiderich and Maroun 2017). Indeed, a few years ago, the scenarios were only just operational; today, one aims to write scenarios which are as real as possible in order to reproduce a crisis situation.

Defining crisis objectives for exercises is thus a step forward. Nevertheless, it is necessary to provide reliable support to the scriptwriter in order to insert the characteristics of a crisis into the scenarios.

Crisis stimuli can be based on lessons learnt from past crises to identify the types and kinetics of the events that crisis managers have faced. These events, their characteristics and frequency could be inserted in crisis exercises. It is also relevant to pay attention to the methods used in the artistic field (Cotte 2014; Lavandier 2014) to inject these types of characteristics into the film or theater scenarios.

Therefore, it is necessary to analyze the cause of surprise, uncertainty, ambiguity, wrong tracks, breakdowns, disturbances or stress in order to reproduce them in the scenarios. When the cause is identified, it becomes easy for the writer to insert the characteristics of a crisis. For example, sources of ambiguity may emerge:

– at the informational level: the information given by the services or by data acquisition systems, the mass of information, the language being used;

– from misunderstanding stakeholders' functions, goals, coordination or behavior;

– at the situation level: ignorance or misunderstanding of facts, expectations, potential developments.

More specifically, if the scriptwriter wishes to insert ambiguity at the informational level, they can insert two opposite or different pieces of information which are both legitimate (e.g. the results of two calculation models).

As for objectives, the number and quality of crises' stimuli must be limited with regard to the profile of the participants. Thus, after inserting all the stimuli, the scriptwriter must check several parameters and validation criteria of the created scenario.

3.4.8. *Verify and validate the pedagogical scriptwriting*

In order to verify educational scriptwriting, the scriptwriter must consider several components of the script:

– its structure: the coherence between events (Bernard 2014) (logic and time dependence, for example); potential omissions and the sequence of stimuli must be examined;

– its credibility: will the participants consider the events as credible? If the answer is no, why and what may be modified?

– its level of difficulty and dynamics: this corresponds to the impact scores over time of the issues, phenomena and all the stimuli that address the objectives;

– its staging and immersion: can the scenario be fictitiously implemented during the exercise (e.g. dummies to simulate victims)?

– involvement of participants: are all participants regularly involved in the exercise?

The training manager of the participating crisis organization or other third parties should also verify the scenario (Borglund and Öberg 2014). When the script is verified, scriptwriters should explain it to animators and observers.

3.4.9. *Prepare the scenario for animators and observers*

In this last stage of scripting, it is necessary to translate the events in such a way that they can be directly transmitted by the animators during the exercise and correctly solicit the targeted objectives. In addition, it is also relevant to propose to the animators a list of recall/redundant stimuli if the trainers want to implicitly request an unattained objective for a second time (Dieudonné and Poumay 2008).

This action will help to define answers to questions that participants may ask during the training. However, animators will need an evaluation during the exercise to determine if the objective has been met. It is therefore necessary to present the scenario to observers well in advance of the exercise so that they can establish performance criteria for overcoming obstacles related to the objectives. They will thus be able to focus their attention on the receivers of the stimulus when it appears. As a result, observers will be able to advise the animators whether it is necessary to further solicit the objective. In addition, observers can provide a relevant look at the stimuli of the script and, in agreement with the scriptwriters, modify the stimuli in order to make a better evaluation.

3.5. Conclusion

A crisis exercise scenario corresponds to the description of the events facing which the participants will have to react to, will be trained for and evaluated on. A pedagogical scenario must solicit targeted training objectives and be able to be adaptable in real time according to the reactions and responses of participants.

The research we have carried out on challenges concerning pedagogical scriptwriting has succeeded in removing certain difficulties for the scriptwriter and ensuring the development of crisis units' skills.

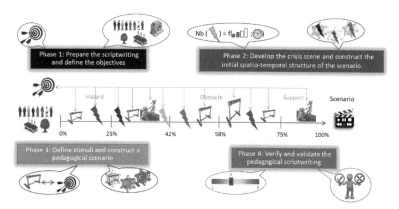

Figure 3.2. *The stages of scriptwriting with the representation of a pedagogical scenario. For a color version of this figure, see www.iste.co.uk/sauvagnargues/crisis.zip*

Indeed, we have identified stages of pedagogical scriptwriting for crisis exercises and defined several specific tools for the scriptwriter as criteria for evaluating the scenario (Figure 3.2). Our research work has therefore led to the definition of several stimuli: stimuli soliciting operational objectives, crises, redundant stimuli and support stimuli.

This research may therefore contribute to improving training in crisis management through the enrichment of methods and means for pedagogical scriptwriting.

However, there is a need for more research and development, both considering further development of the scenario and the evaluation of the design process (Borglund and Öberg 2014). It is also possible to improve the organization (quantity and occurrence) of stimuli within the scenario in order to develop its structure and get closer to a crisis dynamic.

3.6. References

ADPSA (2016). Guide pratique pour rédiger un scénario pédagogique. Available: http://www.adpsa12.org/ADPSA_modele/DOC_PDF/DI_Guid e_Pratique_scenario_pedagogique.pdf [Accessed 11 January 2016].

Bernard, L. (2014). *Guide pratique de formation par la simulation*. VA Press, Versailles.

Borglund, E.A.M. and Öberg, L.-M. (2014). Creation of an exercise scenario: a collaborative design effort. *Proceedings of the 11th International ISCRAM Conference*, May, 488–492.

Cohen, M.S., Freeman, J.T., and Thompson, B. (1998). Critical thinking skills in tactical decision making: a model and a training strategy. In *Decision-Making Under Stress: Implications for Training & Simulation*, Canon-Bowers, J. and Salas, E. (eds). American Psychological Association Publications, Washington, DC.

Cook, D. (2006). Safety and training. *Free flight – The Journal of the Soaring Association of Canada*, 3(6), 16–17.

Combalbert, L. (2005). *Le Management des situations de crise. Anticiper les risques et gérer les crises*. ESF éditeur, Paris.

Combalbert, L. and Delbecque, É. (2012). *La gestion de crise*. PUF, Paris.

Cotte, O. (2014). *Écrire pour le cinéma et la télévision. Structure du scénario, outils et nouvelles techniques d'écriture créative*. Dunod, Paris.

Dieudonné, L. and Poumay, M. (2008). *Le Modèle des Evénements d'Apprentissage – Enseignement*, LabSET-IFR.

Direction de la Défense et de la Sécurité Civiles (2005). Plan Communal de Sauvegarde: Guide pratique d'élaboration. Ministère de l'intérieur et de l'aménagement du territoire.

Direction de la Sécurité Civile (2009). Exercices de Sécurité Civile: Guide thématique sur les exercices PPI. Ministère de l'intérieur, de l'outre-mer et des collectivités territoriales, p. 80.

Driskell, J.E. and Johnston, J.H. (1998). Stress exposure training. In *Making Decisions Under Stress: Implications for Individual and Team Training*, Cannon-Bowers J.A. and Salas E. (eds). American Psychological Association, Washington, DC.

El-Kechai, H. (2008). Conception Collective de scénarios pédagogiques dans un contexte de réingénierie : une approche par la métamodélisation située. Informatique [cs]. University of Maine, France. Available: https://tel.archives-ouvertes.fr/tel-00343203/document.

Fagel, M.J. (2014). *Crisis Management and Emergency Planning: Preparing for Today's Challenges*. CRC Press Taylor and Francis Group.

Federal Emergency Management Agency (2017). Course: IS-120.a – An Introduction to Exercises Lesson 4: Design and Development. Available: https://emilms.fema.gov/IS120A/module4.htm [Accessed 20 December 2017].

Fowlkes, J., Dwyer, D.J., Oser, R.L. and Salas, E. (1998). Event-based approach to training (EBAT). *Int. J. Aviat. Psychol.*, 8(3), 209–222.

Gaultier-Gaillard, S., Persin, M. and Vraie, B. (2012). *Gestion de crise – Les exercices de simulation : de l'apprentissage à l'alerte.* AFNOR, La Plaine Saint-Denis.

Heiderich, D. (2010). *Plan de gestion de crise: organiser, gérer et communiquer en situation de crise.* Dunod, Paris.

Heiderich, D. and Maroun, N. (2017). La mise en récit des exercices de crise. Article de fond dans la LIREC, Newsletter, l'Institut national des hautes études de la sécurité et de la justice (INHESJ), July 2017.

Institut des Risques Majeurs (2008). Mémento Exercices Plan Communal de Sauvegarde. Grenoble.

Lagadec, P. (2015). *Le continent des imprévus – Journal de bord des temps chaotiques.* Les Belles Lettres, Paris.

Lapierre, D. (2016). Méthode EVADE : Une approche intégrée pour l'EValuation et l'Aide au DEbriefing. University of Nîmes, France. Available: https://tel.archives-ouvertes.fr/tel-01695574/document

Lavandier, Y. (2014). *La dramaturgie, l'art du récit.* Le Clown & L'enfant.

Limousin, P. (2017). Contribution à la scénarisation pédagogique d'exercices de crise. PhD Thesis, University of Lyon, L'École des Mines de Saint-Etienne.

O'connor, P., Hörmann, H., Flin, R., Lodge, M. and Goeters, K.M. (2002). The U.S. Navy's Crew Resource Management program: The past present, and recommendations for the future. *Int. J. Aviat. Psychol.,* 12(3), 263–286.

Rankin, A., Kovordanyi, R., Field, J.N., Morin, M., Jenvald, J. and Erikson, H. (eds) (2011). A scenario-based modelling method for simulation systems. In *Proceedings of ISCRAM 2011,* May 8–11, Lisbon, Portugal.

Robert, B. (2002). Nouvelles pratiques pour le pilotage des situations de crise: dix ruptures pour passer d'une logique de procédures à l'apprentissage de la surprise. *Environnement, Risques & Santé,* 1(1), 22–30.

Department of Energy Office of Transportation and Emergency Management (2002). Guidance for Planning, Conducting and Evaluating Transportation Emergency Preparedness Tabletops, Drills and Exercises. Prepared for the Department of Energy Office of Transportation and Emergency Management, p. 46. Available: https://www.energy.gov/sites/prod/files/em/TEPP/4-a-1GuidanceforPlanningExercises.pdf

Villiot-Leclercq, E. (2006). *Capitaliser, diffuser, réutiliser l'expertise pédagogique pour la conception de scénarios pédagogiques: des outils et des méthodes pour enrichir les pratiques dans un contexte d'enseignement à distance* [Online]. Available: https://edutice.archives-ouvertes.fr/edutice-00001416v1/document

Elaboration of Tools to Facilitate the Scenario Development of Crisis Management Training

4.1. Introduction

A crisis may have important consequences, whether at the human, material or economic level. While regulation is an important lever for organizations to be prepared to confront major events through the implementation of plans and procedures, feedback is also stimulating to implement crisis management exercises. Among the different types of crisis exercises, simulations enable crisis units to test their organization and to gain experience (Goutx 2014). In order to implement simulation, it is necessary to develop a scenario that is credible (Boin et al. 2004; Dautun et al. 2011), educational (Baubion et al. 2014a) and interactive at the same time (Barot et al. 2013; Barot 2014), so as to encourage trainees to immerse themselves in a situation that seems realistic and allows them to acquire knowledge, skills and experience. This scenario is implemented by a team of facilitators, also known as a facilitation team (Fréalle et al. 2017). Facilitators are then led to share scripted messages with trainees and

Chapter written by Noémie Fréalle, Florian Tena-Chollet and Sophie Sauvagnargues.

to encourage interaction with them. Here, we are interested in the resources of these facilitators for the implementation of credible, educational and interactive scenarios.

4.2. State of the art

In order to run a script, it is possible to proceed methodically and make use of computer tools. In the specialized literature, it is possible to observe a trend: the execution of the script is mainly ensured by a team of facilitators (Boin *et al.* 2004; Dautun 2007; Gregori *et al.* 2009; Verdel *et al.* 2010; Tena-Chollet 2012; Teclemariam *et al.* in Stern 2014; Fréalle *et al.* 2017; November *et al.* 2017). These facilitators have a script prepared in advance and interact with trainees via different vectors of communication: phone, e-mail, social networks, media, fax and voice (Fréalle *et al.* 2017). Facilitators are at the interface between the script and trainees, and the deployment of the scenario is their responsibility. Yet, to our knowledge, there is no methodology which enables facilitators to run a scenario while respecting credibility, pedagogy and interactivity criteria. Nevertheless, some limitations can be observed as regards the implementation of the three criteria.

4.2.1. *The limitations encountered*

4.2.1.1. *The scenario's credibility called into question*

Credibility is the key ingredient for an efficient simulation (Dautun *et al.* 2011) which has to be effective (Boin *et al.* 2004). However, verisimilitude defects are observed, and the credibility of scenarios are called into question by participants (Boin *et al.* 2004; Gaultier-Gaillard *et al.* 2012; Baubion *et al.* 2014a). These credibility defects may be due to:

– inconsistencies due to the initial scenario or to inadequate responses from the facilitation team (DGSCGC 2013);

– anomalies related to a lack of technical data in the scenario or a lack of feedback during simulation (Verdel *et al.* 2010).

The issue of credibility for crisis management training is essential. Verisimilitude bias can penalize trainees during the learning process. For example, we can observe misunderstandings due to unrealistic elements, such as the absence of victims following an event which might have provoked some (DGSCGC 2013). As a result, we can observe that trainees become disengaged from the simulation (Boin *et al.* 2004). If they do not, they may retain response strategies from the simulation which could actually deteriorate crisis management in future situations.

A priori, credibility defects may be encountered at different levels. They can be found in relation to the development of the hazard, the impact on the territory and the stakes involved, the availability of resources, scheduled deadlines or even the choice of representatives. If the facilitator has no other choice than to admit to a credibility bias, it is possible to announce it before the exercise and to incorporate it as a "rule of the game" (November *et al.* 2017). While this does not totally prevent the lack of credibility, it is useful for avoiding the consequences it could have on the educational reach of the simulation.

4.2.1.2. *Restrained educational reach*

A crisis scenario makes trainees familiar with the situation and grants the immersion of participants when it is associated with environmental and contextual elements (Tena-Chollet 2012; Tena-Chollet *et al.* 2016). However, the educational impact of each message is not clearly established. Without calling it into question, it is nonetheless necessary to consider the impact of the scenario on the learning process.

It is often said that educational goals should be determined before the scripting phase. However, there is no existing method for structuring the selection of these objectives and their integration in the scenario. Only recommendations are made, for example, regarding the number of objectives that it is possible to use (Tena-Chollet 2012) or concerning the fact that trainees should not be overloaded, for fear of losing their attention during the exercise (Renger *et al.* 2009). In order to ensure the educational reach of the scenario, the facilitator should draw on their experience as a scriptwriter.

Specialized literature has never made reference to the difficulty of building a scenario which sufficiently values the contribution of each member of the crisis unit. It sometimes happens that in a group of trainees, some feel less involved, and therefore the phenomenon of disengagement emerges.

4.2.1.3. *Rigid scenarios*

At present, the main information available to facilitators is present in the scenario (Verdel *et al.* 2010; Dautun *et al.* 2011; November *et al.* 2017).

The development of crisis scenarios is often interrupted, even before the start of the simulation (Boin *et al.* 2004; Noori *et al.* 2017). The story structure is called into question and might be responsible for the lack of adaptability and interactivity (Mercan *et al.* 2011). Apparently, the most interactive scenarios might be the less developed ones and those in which trainees can freely exchange among each other (Baubion *et al.* 2014b). It can also be observed that this rigid aspect deprives participants of the necessary margin for taking the initiative (Barot 2014). Among basic psychological needs, we can mention the feeling of living an optimal experience and of having our own choices respected or followed (Deci *et al.* 2000, 2008). It is therefore necessary for the scenario to fit the decisions made by trainees.

For others, responsibility is beyond their scope of action. This can be due to the absence of a method for dynamically generating scenarios which focus on coordination and the unexpected (Comes *et al.* 2013; Steelman *et al.* 2013). For Noori *et al.*, the unexpected element is important and should be taken into consideration, since it is necessary to acquire training in handling unusual situations or those situations in which procedures established in plans are not enough (Noori *et al.* 2017). Nevertheless, the rigid aspect of the scenario leaves no room for original behavior and thought (Lagadec 2007; Reason in Noori *et al.* 2017).

It thus becomes necessary to produce more flexible scenarios (Carroll 1999; Mercan *et al.* 2009; Renger *et al.* 2009). In order to adapt the scenario, a possible solution could be to thoroughly understand what participants can initially do and what they are concretely able to accomplish later (Amokrane-Ferka *et al.* 2013). A way of anticipating the actions of participants is to adopt the *brainstorming* technique. However, it is not possible to predict everything, because people interpret their experience and adjust their perception based on these interpretations (Nisbett *et al.* 1977; Renger *et al.* 2009). This bias induces a reconstruction of reality that is often ill-equipped for identifying dysfunctions (Carroll 1999). Expecting to anticipate all the decisions that trainees may make is laborious and illusory and leads to screenwriting instability (Carroll 2000).

The real challenge is therefore to find a structure that makes it possible to control the scenario, but without providing all the possibilities. In order to meet this requirement, Szilas proposes to delinearize the scenario. In addition, he suggests no longer apprehending the scenario as a chronological sequence of events (Szilas *et al.* 2003). However, once the idea has been submitted, he admits that the intellectual process is still complex.

4.2.1.4. *The impact of the human factor in the implementation of the scenario*

After having studied the limits of credibility, pedagogy and interactivity, it is possible to address the organizational boundaries regarding the execution of the crisis scenario. In the same way it occurs with crisis management, the human factor is essential for managing facilitation. In fact, facilitators experience the same uncertainties, time pressure and management of the unexpected as crisis managers during a major event. Therefore, it is clear that in crisis units, we are often pushed to manage situations that are similar to a real crisis (Verdel *et al.* 2010). Also, as in crisis units, it is possible to observe that there are communication problems between facilitators. Several elements may be the cause: the importance of the number of requests by trainees, the lack of methodology, the complex use of a technology platform, the spatial organization of the animation team or even the number of facilitators.

4.2.2. Analogy with interactive narratives

To overcome the limits identified in terms of credibility, pedagogy and interactivity, here we suggest resorting to an analogy between the facilitation of a crisis scenario and interactive drama. Drawing an analogy between interactive narratives and crisis scenarios makes it possible to identify similarities between one and the other. It is by discerning the similarities that it seems possible to determine which strategies used in interactive narratives could be adapted to counteract the previously identified limitations in scriptwriting.

Szilas defines interactive narratives as "a narrative genre on computers where the user is one main character in the story and the other characters and events are automated through a program written by an author. Being a character means choosing all narrative actions of this character" (Szilas 2007). It is a tool that should both offer freedom to the player in terms of action and ensure that the story the scriptwriter has written is unfolded in a consistent manner (Riedl *et al.* 2006; Barot 2014).

The interactive narrative is not only used in video games but also found in various media such as theater and documentaries (Shilkrot *et al.* 2014). We also encounter an interactive narrative in texts based on interactive fiction or "choose your own adventure" books (Mateas *et al.* 2002a; Barot 2014). Conventional narrative forms such as those used in novels or movies do not solve the problems of consistency and control which are necessary for the interactive narratives, due to the passive status of the observer (Riedl *et al.* 2003). Shilkrot even claims that video games have the most similarities with computer-assisted interactive narratives, in terms of graphics and the interactivity produced by artificial intelligence (Shilkrot *et al.* 2014). Besides, it is the use of artificial intelligence that makes it possible to create a narrative manager for handling the story in real time, according to the choice of players. We can therefore ask ourselves, what the value of an interactive narrative architecture is and whether it actually contributes to grant freedom to the player, while preserving the coherence of the story.

4.2.2.1. The master facilitator and the narrative manager

Whether it is the master facilitator of a crisis management training exercise – also known as the exercise coordinator (Dautun *et al.* 2011) – or the narrative manager of an interactive narrative system (Marsella *et al.* 2000; Mateas *et al.* 2002b; Riedl *et al.* 2003; Mott *et al.* 2006; Si *et al.* 2007; Szilas 2007), their mission is to ensure the consistent unfolding of the scenario, and, if necessary, to influence it following the criteria of consistency or its goals. Yet, their methodology differs in how they carry out their mission. The narrative manager appeals to a logic established using algorithms (Si *et al.* 2007; Szilas 2007; Barot 2014), whereas the master facilitator draws on his/her experience and discernment.[1] The master facilitator should be allowed to work in the same conditions. In addition, it is not necessary for the master facilitator to have thorough knowledge of everything that is happening, but to be in contact only with those needed for orchestrating the scenario in a credible and interactive way.

4.2.2.2. Facilitators, a dynamic, but troubled interface

The main difference between the interactive narrative and crisis scenarios is the interface that exists between users and the narrative manager. In interactive narrative structures, a human–machine interface makes it possible to feed the narrative manager with users' choices (Mateas *et al.* 2005; Si *et al.* 2005; Mott *et al.* 2006). The structure of the interface does not affect data feeding the narrative manager. The latter reacts impartially in view of the elements in its possession or the algorithms that make it up (Si *et al.* 2007; Szilas 2007; Barot 2014). For the crisis scenario, this is different, because it is the facilitators who collect the choices of trainees. Thus, they are confronted with a difficulty: they have to respond to these choices in an adapted and almost immediate way. Despite being transmitted to the master facilitator and validated by him/her, the responses contributed by facilitators are sometimes subjective. In this case, the executive processes, which do not fit into a formal frame, risk providing differing answers in identical contexts.

---

1 Taken from the observations of crisis simulations carried out in the context of thesis research (Fréalle 2018).

Another difficulty that facilitators may encounter is due to their more or less incomplete knowledge of the characters they are simulating. In interactive narrative systems, the authors provide everything that should be known about the characters (Riedl *et al.* 2003). From there, the computing system identifies the necessary knowledge to be mobilized and can use it effectively. The human factor makes the operation different when people perform the animation and simulate the characters. It is necessary to allow scenario facilitators to access knowledge by providing them with the elements required. It is also a question of organizing this knowledge and providing the necessary indications in order not to jeopardize the credibility of the scenario or its educational reach.

4.2.2.3. *Individual or group learning*

The interactive narrative involves a human–machine interface that is designed for one individual. For crisis management training, it is necessary to understand the training at group scale, since these groups, the crisis units, are the ones that will manage crises. The shift from the individual to the group sphere creates a scale difficulty. The information about what participants do is distributed among all the facilitators and does not go through a single circuit. In fact, unlike interactive storytelling, where there is a single circuit between the scenario and the participant, there are various circuits in crisis management training. If the interactive narrative process is difficult to set up for a single participant, we imagine that it can be rather difficult to implement for a group.

4.2.2.4. *Contribution of the interactive narrative to improve facilitation*

Everything is interconnected in the interactive narrative structure: the world of history, the actions of the players, the behavior of characters and the narrative logic. Therefore, it seems reasonable to offer facilitators the opportunity to share the elements which are necessary to the scenario's interactivity.

The analogy between interactive narrative and the crisis scenario makes it possible to identify the elements that should be made available to facilitators for them to successfully carry out their mission:

– provide the master facilitator with sufficient knowledge for him/her to orchestrate the scenario. These elements will have to be identified and organized;

– reinforce the evolutionary process of the scenario by providing facilitators with the elements they will need. It will also be necessary to identify and organize these elements. This point also helps to increase the credibility of the scenario and its pedagogical reach;

– provide facilitators with the opportunity to share their knowledge concerning the scenario in progress. This makes it possible to counterbalance the dissolution of information at a group scale.

4.3. Method

To meet the previously identified needs, we propose considering facilitation aids so as to support facilitators in carrying out their task. As part of the analogy between the interactive narrative and the facilitation of crisis scenarios, previously identified elements should be concretely harmonized with facilitation tools. Here, we can identify two tools that should be made available to facilitators: a facilitation form and a shared facilitation support.

4.3.1. *Facilitation form*

4.3.1.1. *Structure of the facilitation form*

The facilitation form is an aid which should help the facilitator to play his/her role in the context of the simulated scenario. It is therefore complementary to the scenario. In the form, the facilitator should be able to find all the necessary information to interact with trainees. Its first purpose is to provide the facilitator with enough elements to be credible. The second objective ensures that the elements are consistent with the scenario in order to guarantee the educational reach of the learning situation. Finally, the third objective is that the structure of the facilitation form helps the facilitator to quickly find the data he/she needs at the moment of the simulation.

We can identify three types of data which are necessary for the facilitator:

– Contextual data: these are data strictly linked to the role. Thus, we can find the patronym, the setting where the character is found and, if applicable, the human, material and logistical resources.

– Data related to the major mission that the crisis unit has to solve, assumed by trainees. The nature of the mission will vary depending on the type of crisis unit (industrial, local, departmental or national). It is important to identify the type of mission in order to structure data in an intelligible way. Every large mission (e.g. the alert) can be broken down into several actions. Then, it is possible to characterize these actions by describing the following traits: (1) those likely to implement the action, (2) the place where the actions unfold or the beneficiaries of such an action, (3) the action's implementation period and (4) the required resources for carrying it out. Depending on the action, it may also be relevant to specify other elements.

– Data related to the scripted events. In fact, facilitators need data that do not fall within the missions assumed by the crisis unit. These data are related to the disruptive events injected into the scenario. If these events concern the role simulated by the facilitator, this should be specified in the facilitation form: the background of this event, the consequences that should be taken into consideration and, if it is known, the response that the communal crisis unit should give.

Figure 4.1 specifies all of the elements that should be informed by the facilitation form established for each role.

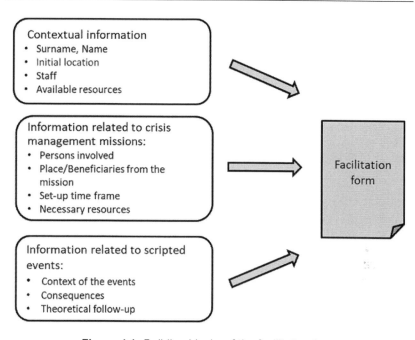

Figure 4.1. *Building blocks of the facilitation form*

4.3.1.2. *Development of role forms to be used in an exercise*

Once we have identified the type of information that the facilitator should find in their facilitation form, it is necessary to establish how this can be developed in a practical way.

For this purpose, it is necessary to use two types of resources: (1) everything related to regulation and habitual practices and (2) crisis management plans, implemented for the crisis unit. Therefore, it is necessary to analyze data in order to identify (1) the roles considered as well as those that will have to be simulated, (2) the responsibilities of each of these roles and their habits, (3) the missions and actions that the simulated roles are likely to carry out, either on request of the crisis unit simulated by trainees or not, and (4) the human, material and logistical resources that each of these roles has at its disposal. Figure 4.2 thus summarizes the possible ways to create facilitation forms.

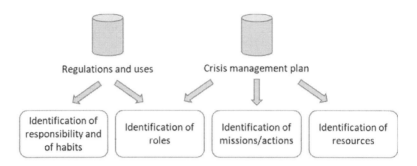

Figure 4.2. *Managing information for filling out facilitation forms*

4.3.2. *Management of facilitation data*

During simulation, facilitators are invited to exchange information. It is possible to distinguish two types of information (Fréalle 2018): information transmitted to trainees and information produced by the facilitator, following the decisions made by trainees. As regards the information produced by facilitators, we can establish a distinction between information prepared before the simulation and information improvised during the simulation. The facilitation form, which was previously introduced, enables facilitators to have the maximum amount of pre-established information and to reduce improvisation by facilitators. However, facilitators have to manage a lot of information, in the same way as the members of a crisis unit. We can identify four types of problems related to poor information management: unverified information, mistakenly transmitted information, information inappropriate that is for matching pre-established educational objectives and late information. These problems may have more or less general consequences on the quality of the scenario. Credibility might be undermined, or the educational reach and the scenario's interactivity might be altered.

In terms of management of facilitation-related information, the challenge is to have access to the right information at the right time. In view of the large amount of information that needs to be exchanged, it seems necessary to make access to information easier for facilitators. In order to make information more accessible, we suggest the development of an information flow diagram within the facilitation process, so as to master its sequencing. Two main steps are identified to elaborate this model: identifying the information that needs to circulate within the facilitation and the development of information flow diagrams.

4.3.2.1. Identification of the facilitation information flow

Before producing an information flow diagram at the core of the facilitation process, it is necessary to spot the kind of information that circulates effectively. To do this, it is necessary to have determined the roles that should be played by facilitators, in advance. It is then necessary to distinguish the missions which are likely to be addressed for each of these roles, as well as the actions related to these missions. For each of these actions, the necessary information for the role has to be defined. At this stage, we can identify five types of information: (1) the actors involved in the implementation of the action, (2) the place affected by the action or its beneficiaries, (3) the time frame or the duration, as well as the status of the action (requested, underway, completed), (4) the details which characterize the action and (5) the resources mobilized for carrying it out.

Figure 4.3 schematizes this stage.

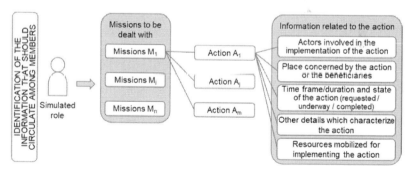

Figure 4.3. *Process for identifying the information that circulates within the facilitation meeting*

At the end of this first stage, it is possible to account for the necessary information for each simulated role. *A fortiori*, after having distributed the roles to the members of the facilitation team (Fréalle *et al.* 2017), we can establish the necessary information to each facilitator.

4.3.2.2. *Formulation of information flow diagrams*

In this second stage of modeling the information flow within the facilitation process, the idea is to describe all of the six steps necessary for formulating information flow diagrams. The first step is to sketch all of the actions that may be implemented by the roles simulated during the facilitation process. The second step should make it possible to determine the roles affected by each piece of information, so as to decide which information flow should be established. For this purpose, we may distinguish between two possible groups of roles: those implementing the action and those benefiting from such an action. After having established the different flow channels needed between roles, we must decide on the kind of information that should circulate through these channels. Starting from the work done in the first stage, it is necessary to identify what kind of information needs to be exchanged for each action and between the different groups of roles. We thus obtain an information flow diagram for each identified action. However, information can be similar from one action to another. Besides, there may be a large number of identified actions, and it is interesting to rationalize the modeling of the information flow. The fifth step merges information flow diagrams produced for each action with the major missions previously defined for identifying the flow of information circulating within the facilitation. The last step distinguishes information which can be prepared beforehand from that which can be produced during the simulation. This makes it possible to (1) ensure that facilitation forms contain all the information which can be previously established and (2) identify the information which can be produced and exchanged by facilitators during the simulation. Figure 4.4 illustrates these different steps.

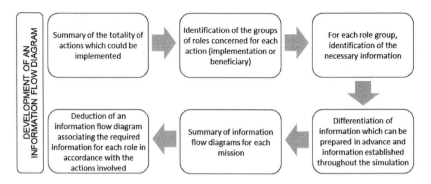

Figure 4.4. *Process for modeling the flow of information within the facilitation exercise*

Information flow diagrams within the facilitation process make it possible to establish the kind of information that needs to be exchanged and the roles affected by this information exchange. It is therefore possible to streamline such exchanges among the members of the facilitation team.

4.4. Results

The method for managing facilitation-related information was implemented for exercises at the communal level – trainees were encouraged to simulate a municipal crisis unit. In this section, we will present a facilitation form for the role of a technical field team leader, the ways in which the facilitator can use it and an information flow diagram for the lockdown mission.

4.4.1. *Facilitation form for the technical field team leader*

For a simulation of a crisis at the communal level, a total of 24 roles must be simulated (Fréalle 2018). Here, we choose to introduce a role belonging to a low facilitation level (Fréalle *et al.* 2017): the communal technical field team leader implementing all the actions related to the technical services. The facilitation form enables the facilitator to contextualize their role, thanks to the elements mentioned in the "general information" section. Then, for each of the missions identified at the communal level (alert, lockdown, evacuation, accommodation, safety and post-crisis), the facilitator can find actions which the crisis unit is likely to ask him/her to implement within the context of the crisis simulation. For example, if trainees decide to implement a lockdown measure, the safety field team leader will be contacted *a priori* in order to support the containment perimeter at this school. In addition to the facilitation form, a monitoring chart of the resources deployed is made available to the facilitator.

General information	Contact name from the technical field team	Emmanuel(le) DUBOIS
	Available staff	Four agents, including you
	Staff position at the outset	In a meeting at the technical pole (*address*)
	Available resources	Two light vehicles Road signs (at the technical pole – *address*)
Alert	Reception of the alert	Must be informed by the technical leader present at the crisis unit
Lockdown	Request for support for school lockdown – the safety field team may be concerned (*a priori* not requested)	– **Resources:** two agents + contribution of adhesive tape and wet cloths – **Duration:** 10 minutes to arrive on scene and 5 minutes for the intervention – **Difficulties**: respiratory + staff and resources management
Evacuation	Leading response teams to the premises	– **Where**: southern access (*address*) – **Resources:** two people/one car – **Duration:** 10 minutes to arrive on the scene and intervention until reception of counter-order – **Difficulties**: staff and resources management
Accommodation	Not concerned (for simplification reasons)	

Safety procedures	Road rehabilitation (sidewalks, public lighting and out of order red lights)	– **Where:** at the level of the accident – *address* – **Resources:** two agents + one vehicle – **Duration**: 1 hour – **Difficulties**: staff and resource management
	Installation of proper warning signs (in collaboration with the field safety team)	– **Where:** place of the accident/safety perimeter/retreat position/shelter – **Resources:** panels + two agents + one vehicle – **Duration:** 5 minutes to get to the place and 2 minutes for setting up – **Difficulties**: staff and resource management
	Closure of (water/gas) networks in communal establishments open to the public (EOPs)	– **Where:** school, social rehabilitation center – **Resources:** two agents + one vehicle – **Duration**: trip duration (immediate if already present on the spot or 10 minutes, and then 10 more minutes for implementation)
Post-crisis	Revamping of water, electricity networks	– **Where:** Louis Leprince Ringuet school – **Resources:** two to four people – **Duration:** 15/30 minutes per building (depending on the total number of persons involved)

Table 4.1. *Facilitation form for the technical field team leader implemented during a crisis simulation*

A post-exercise questionnaire is submitted to facilitators at the end of the crisis simulation. In this questionnaire, facilitators are requested in particular to offer feedback regarding the facilitation forms. During a crisis simulation that aimed to validate the method, six facilitators who worked on facilitation forms expressed their satisfaction. It was found that the information was useful, making it possible to better understand and characterize roles, and to have the necessary contextual elements for role facilitation. Therefore, implementing the facilitation form is important for the proper functioning of facilitation.

4.4.2. The "lockdown" mission's information flow diagram used in a simulation exercise at the communal level

For each of the missions identified in the context of communal crisis simulation (alert, lockdown, evacuation, accommodation, safety and post-crisis), information flow diagrams were produced, based on the methodological elements previously introduced. In order to explain what these models correspond to, the model of the "lockdown" mission is introduced here (Figure 4.5). We can distinguish between two groups of roles involved in this mission: those who materially support the lockdown and the ones who are confined. When the members of the communal crisis unit decide to confine an area, they can ask three actors for support: the telephone company, firefighters and the safety and technical field team leaders. It is therefore necessary for these three roles to know the challenges present in the confinement perimeter, the prescribed period for the lockdown, the status of the action as well as the resources they will have to mobilize in order to mitigate the challenges of confinement. Apart from the status of the action which cannot be anticipated by the scenario writer, all of this information can be prepared before the simulation.

For the second group, the roles confined to a certain area may be the emergency shelter team leader, who may be encouraged to contain the emergency shelter, as well as the EOP leaders, and the residents present in the area to be confined. Once affected by a lockdown instruction, holders of these roles also need to know the number of people involved (if there are other people present with them), as well as their degree of vulnerability. They also need to know the duration of the lockdown provided by the authorities, the state of the action, as well as the resources that will be available to them during the confinement.

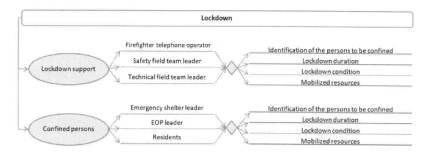

Figure 4.5. *Information flow diagram for the "lockdown" mission*

Such an information flow diagram makes it possible to identify clear roles and, *a fortiori,* facilitators, who must exchange information among themselves, as well as agree on the type of information needed. For the diagrams to be of use, it is also important to observe that:

– the formulation of information must be accurate. Indeed, regardless of the category of information, it is important that this is clear enough. Subsequently, information that may generate confusion or other interpretations can impair the credibility of the scenario;

– information should be disseminated quickly and simultaneously among all facilitators. This enables each facilitator to have access to the necessary information and to be consistent regarding the data disseminated during the simulation. This contributes both to the interactivity and the credibility of the scenario.

Good information flow favors easy access to information for all facilitators. The facilitation team has the necessary elements at hand to make a decision that will impact on the evolution of the scenario in line with the pre-established educational goals. The structure of the scenario is no longer rigid; facilitators can consider more possibilities and actually offer a suitable and tailor-made simulation to trainees.

4.5. Conclusion and perspectives

In order to overcome the scriptwriting limitations encountered in terms of credibility, pedagogy and interactivity, we propose the development of a method to better manage information during facilitation exercises. To do this, it is important to identify the information that needs to be prepared before the crisis simulation and to structure the exchange of information between facilitators during the exercise. As a first step, we suggest a methodology for developing facilitation forms, including the accompanying responsibilities, actions and resources for each simulated role. To structure the facilitation form, we suggest compartmentalizing the facilitation form in three sections: the contextual elements, the elements related to missions that a communal crisis unit should lead and the elements related to the disruptive scripted events.

Second, we propose the development of an information flow diagram within the facilitation exercise. This resource identifies the information that facilitators need and the exchange flow that should be implemented. Indeed, it does not seem satisfactory to provide all the information together, but rather to sequence it. After identifying all the information managed for each role simulated during the facilitation exercise, information flow diagrams are offered based on the major missions that the crisis unit assumed by trainees has to handle.

In order to illustrate these methods, we introduce a facilitation form and an information flow diagram deployed for a crisis simulation at the communal level.

To effectively implement information flow diagrams within the facilitation exercise, it seems necessary to propose a collaborative support for facilitators. It is also necessary to validate these methodological elements in the context of other crisis simulations, on several critical scales (industrial, local, regional and national).

4.6. References

Amokrane-Ferka, K., Lourdeaux, D., and Michel, G. (2013). Tracking and dynamic scenario adaptation system in virtual environment. In *Artificial Intelligence in Education*, Lane, H.C., Yacef, K., Mostow, J. and Pavlik, P. (eds). Springer, Berlin, Heidelberg.

Barot, C. (2014). Scénarisation d'environnements virtuels. Vers un équilibre entre contrôle, cohérence et adaptabilité. PhD Thesis, University of Technology, Compiègne.

Barot, C., Lourdeaux, D., and Lenne, D. (2013). Dynamic scenario adaptation balancing control, coherence and emergence. *Proceedings of the 5th International Conference on Agents and Artificial Intelligence (ICAART)*, Barcelona. doi:10.5220/0004213802320237.

Baubion, C. and Radisch, J. (2014a). Toolkit background paper. *4th Meeting of the OECD High Level Risk Forum*, Paris.

Baubion, C. and Jacobzone, S. (2014b). Strategic crisis management exercises: Challenges and design tools. *4th Meeting of the OECD High Level Risk Forum*, Paris. Available: http://www.oecd.org /officialdocuments/publicdisplaydocumentpdf/?cote=GOV/PGC/HLRF(2 014)9&docLanguage=En

Boin, A., Kofman-Bos, C., and Overdijk, W. (2004). Crisis simulations: Exploring tomorrow's vulnerabilities and threats. *Simul. Gaming*, 35(3), 378–393. doi:10.1177/1046878104266220.

Carroll, J.M. (1999). Designing and using simulations and role-play exercises. *Proceedings of the 32nd Hawaii International Conference on System Sciences*, Hawaii.

Carroll, J.M. (2000). Five reasons for scenario-based design. *Interact. Comput.*, 13(1), 43–60. doi:10.1016/S0953-5438(00)00023-0.

Comes, T., Bertsch, V., and French, S. (2013). Designing dynamic stress tests for improved critical infrastructure resilience. *International Conference on Information Systems for Crisis Response and Management (ISCRAM)*, Baden, Germany.

Dautun, C. (2007). Contribution à l'étude des crises de grande ampleur: connaissance et aide à la décision pour la sécurité civile. PhD Thesis, École Nationale Supérieure des Mines, Saint-Etienne.

Dautun, C., Pardini, G., and Roux-Dufort, C. (2011). La formation des acteurs publics à la gestion de crise. Le cas français. *11ème colloque sur la Sécurité Civile*.

Deci, E.L. and Ryan, R.M. (2000). The "what" and "why" of goal pursuits: Human needs and the self-determination of behavior. *Psychol. Inq.*, 11(4), 227–268. doi:10.1207/S15327965PLI1104_01.

Deci, E.L. and Ryan, R.M. (2008). Facilitating optimal motivation and psychological well-being across life's domains. *Can. Psychol.*, 49(1). doi:10.1037/0708-5591.49.3.262.

Direction Générale de la Sécurité Civile et de la Gestion des Crises (2013). Synthèse des retours d'expériences des exercices 2013. Ministère de l'Intérieur.

Fréalle, N. (2018). Formation à la gestion de crise à l'échelle communale: méthode d'élaboration et de mise en œuvre de scénarios de crise crédibles, pédagogiques et interactifs. PhD Thesis, IMT Mines Alès.

Fréalle, N., Tena-Chollet, F., and Sauvagnargues, S. (2017). The key role of animation in the execution of crisis management exercises. In *Proceedings of the 14th International Conference on Information Systems for Crisis Response and Management (ISCRAM)*, Comes, T., Bénaben, F., Hanachi, C., Lauras, M., and Montarnal, A. (eds). Albi, France.

Gaultier-Gaillard, S., Persin, M., and Vraie, B. (2012). *Gestion de crise, les exercices de simulation: de l'apprentissage à l'alerte*. AFNOR.

Goutx, D. (2014). Réaliser la gravité d'enjeux abstraits à travers une simulation: comprendre COP-RW comme un rite de passage. *Négociations*, 22(2), 17–28. doi:10.3917/neg.022.0017

Gregori, N., Brassac, C., and Sirvaut, A. (2009). Appropriation collective d'un dispositif de formation. *Epique'2009*, 73–81.

Lagadec, P. (2007). *Enseigner la question des crises. Enjeux, Obstacles, Initiatives. CECO-1568*, Ecole Polytechnique.

Marsella, S., Johnson, W., and LaBore, C. (2000). Interactive pedagogical drama. In *Proceedings of the Fourth International Conference on Autonomous Agents*, Barcelona, Spain, 301–308. doi:10.1145/336595.337507.

Mateas, M. and Stern, A. (2002a). Towards integrating plot and character for interactive drama. *Socially Intelligent Agents*. Springer, Boston, MA, 221–228. doi:10.1007/0-306-47373-9_27.

Mateas, M. and Stern, A. (2002b). *Architecture, Authorial Idioms and Early Observations of the Interactive Drama Façade*. School of Computer Science, Carnegie Mellon University.

Mateas, M. and Stern, A. (2005). Structuring content in the Façade interactive drama architecture. *AIIDE*, 93–98. doi:10.1.1.101.4192.

Mercan, G., Morizot, C., Chauzel, J.M., and Rannou, G. (2009). Guide thématique sur les exercices PPI. Ministère de l'Intérieur.

Mercan, G., Morizot, C., Chevallier, A., and Rannou, G. (2011). Guide méthodologique sur les exercices cadre et terrain. Ministère de l'Intérieur.

Mott, B.W. and Lester, J.C. (2006). U-director: A decision-theoretic narrative planning architecture for storytelling environments. *Proceedings of the Fifth International Joint Conference on Autonomous Agents and Multiagents Systems*. ACM, 977–984. doi:10.1145/1160633.1160808.

Nisbett, R.E. and Wilson, T.D. (1977). Telling more than we can know: Verbal reports on mental processes. *Psychol. Rev.*, 84(3), 231–259. doi:10.1037/0033-295X.84.3.231.

Noori, N.S., Wang, Y., and Comes, T. (2017). Behind the scenes of scenario-based training: Understanding scenario design and requirements in high-risk and and uncertain environments. *Proceedings of the 14th ISCRAM Conference*, Albi, France.

November, V. and Créton-Cazanave, L. (2017). *La gestion de crise à l'épreuve de l'exercice – EU SEQUANA*. La Documentation française.

Renger, R., Wakelee, J., Bradshaw, J., and Hites, L. (2009). Steps in writing an effective master scenario events list. *J. Emerg. Manag.*, 7(6), 51–60.

Riedl, M.O. and Stern, A. (2006). Believable agents and intelligent story adaptation for interactive storytelling. *International Conference on Technologies for Interactive Digital Storytelling and Entertainment*, Springer, Berlin, Heidelberg, 1–12, December. doi:10.1007/11944577_1.

Riedl, M., Saretto, C.J., and Young, R.M. (2003). Managing interaction between users and agents in a multi-agent storytelling environment. *Proceedings of the Second International Joint Conference on Autonomous Agents and Multiagent Systems*. ACM, 741–748, July. doi:http://doi.acm.org/10.1145/860575.860694.

Shilkrot, R., Montfort, N., and Maes, P. (2014). Narratives of augmented worlds. *Mixed and Augmented Reality-Media, Art, Social Science, Humanities and Design (ISMAR-MASH'D), 2014 IEEE International Symposium*. IEEE, Munich, 35–42. doi:10.1109/ISMAR-AMH.2014. 6935436.

Si, M., Marsella, S.C., and Pynadath, D.V. (2005). Thespian: Using multi-agent fitting to craft interactive drama. *Proceedings of the Fourth International Joint Conference on Autonomous Agents and Multiagent Systems*. ACM, 21–28. doi:10.1145/1082473.1082477.

Si, M., Marsella, S.C.S., and Pynadath, D.D. V. (2007). Proactive authoring for interactive drama: An author's assistant. *International Workshop on Intelligent Virtual Agents*. Springer, Berlin, Heidelberg, 225–237.

Steelman, T.A. and McCaffrey, S. (2013). Best practices in risk and crisis communication: Implications for natural hazards management. *Nat. Hazards*, 65(1), 683–705. doi:10.1007/s11069-012-0386-z.

Stern, E.K. (ed.). (2014). *Designing Crisis Management Training and Exercises for Strategic Leaders*. Försvarshögskolan, Stockholm.

Szilas, N. (2007). A computational model of an intelligent narrator for interactive narratives. *Appl. Artif. Intel.*, 21(8), 753–801. doi:10.1080/08839510701526574.

Szilas, N., Marty, O., and Réty, J.-H. (2003). Authoring highly generative interactive drama. *International Conference on Virtual Storytelling*. Springer, Berlin, Heidelberg. doi:10.1007/978-3-540-40014-1_5.

Tena-Chollet, F. (2012). Elaboration d'un environnement semi-virtuel de formation à la gestion stratégique de crise, basé sur la simulation multi-agents. PhD Thesis, École Nationale Supérieure des Mines, Saint-Etienne.

Tena-Chollet, F., Tixier, J., Dandrieux, A., and Slangen, P. (2016). Training decision-makers: Existing strategies for natural and technological crisis management and specifications of an improved simulation-based tool. *Safety Sci.*, 97, 144–153. doi:10.1016/j.ssci.2016.03.025

Verdel, T., Tardy, A., Lopez, P., Hansen, C., and Deschanels, J. (2010). iCrisisTM: un dispositif original de simulation de gestion de crise. *17e Congrès de Maîtrise des Risques et de Sûreté de Fonctionnement*, La Rochelle, October.

How Can We Evaluate the Participants of a Crisis Management Training Exercise?

5.1. Introduction

Feedback provided on catastrophic events such as Fukushima (Japan, 2011) or AZF (France, 2001) highlighted the complexity of strategic decision-making in emergency situations. Besides, the recurrence of crises in the field of major hazards implies that managing organizations participate in crisis management training exercises in order to develop skills both at the individual and the collective level. The limitations of current training in terms of evaluation and debriefing have prompted us to conduct research on the development of a methodology for assessing and facilitating debriefing, called EVADE (EValuation and Assistance for DEbriefing). This methodology, developed following the observation of 39 exercises, is based on the creation of an educational toolkit that makes it possible to structure and formalize the assessment of skills required in a crisis unit. A total of 192 educational objectives, classified according to three levels of difficulty, make up the educational base frame that must be used by facilitators to structure not only technical expectations but also the organizational aspects necessary for the efficient functioning of a crisis unit during crisis

Chapter written by Dimitri LAPIERRE, Florian TENA-CHOLLET, Jérôme TIXIER, Aurélia BONY-DANDRIEUX and Karine WEISS.

management. Observation and assessment tools are set up to conduct real-time assessment of trainees during the simulation exercises in crisis management. What is more, they allow a dynamic assessment that, based on the follow-up of the educational objectives of the exercise, makes it possible to interactively adapt the scenario to the performance of trainees in real time.

Crisis management in the field of major risks depends on the strategic response offered by managing organizations. In fact, the crisis response procedure, commonly known as "crisis unit", aims to implement anticipatory, vigilance and intervention measures (Lachtar 2012). Due to its suddenness, the appearance of a crisis makes decision-making complex and fills it with urgency and uncertainty (Crocq *et al.* 2009). In all cases, the situation requires decision-makers to provide strategic responses under stress (Dautun 2007). One of the main difficulties faced by these teams lies in the fact that they are ephemeral: because of the rarity of these events, these teams are only activated when a crisis actually takes place (Dautun and Lacroix 2013). The specificity of this top decision-making place, which is both structured and highly hierarchical, presents a serious risk, that of isolation, especially due to its remoteness from the terrain and its compartmentalization (Maisonneuve 2010). Given the complexity of the first moments of a crisis, it is essential for crisis managers to be better prepared to be surprised when confronted with unforeseen situations during training (Lagadec 2012). This training comprises the organization of exercises, making it possible to simulate a crisis situation and therefore to activate the crisis unit (Gaultier-Gaillard *et al.* 2012). It is through these scenarios that crisis managers will be able to gain experience, improve their level of expertise and teamwork-related skills (Sayegh *et al.* 2004; Heiderich 2010). By contrast, for crisis managers to develop their ability to better adapt to these situations which encourage them to make decisions under stress, this requires the organization of crisis management training, focusing on both technical and organizational aspects (Salas and Cannon-Bowers 1997; Fowlkes *et al.* 1998). The objective of this chapter is to formalize the assessment and observation of participants in crisis management training exercises, both on technical and non-technical (organizational) aspects. In addition, observers and facilitators can use this information during the debriefing phase.

5.2. Review

From a pedagogical point of view, conducting training exercises based on simulations is considered to be the most immersive way of learning (Gaba 2004). This observation is shared in different fields, ranging from the medical field to aeronautics. Classically, a simulation exercise is made up of several steps: it starts with briefing (a reminder of the roles and missions of each participant, a presentation of the triggering event and its context), followed by the exercise (deployment of a scenario previously built, thanks to the interactions of facilitators), and debriefing takes place later (discussions and analysis around the observations made during simulation) (Beaubien and Baker 2004; Gaultier-Gaillard et al. 2012). The performance of this type of exercise provides opportunities for trainees to learn by putting their special skills into practice (Kosarzycki et al. 2002; Raybourn 2005). In addition, this allows them to engage in a dynamic behavioral process, while being involved in an environment which is simultaneously immersive, contextualized and, most of all, realistic (Power et al. 2013).

While it is true that the performance of this type of exercise has multiple advantages for crisis managers, it is nonetheless important to conduct debriefing effectively; indeed, the trainee needs to analyze what was done throughout the exercise. Regardless of whether this analysis concerns the whole group or, on the contrary, whether it is performed at the individual level, restitution implies an assessment of trainees based on the different educational objectives set for the training (Ramspacher 2013). A pedagogical objective implies wondering "what should trainees be able to do?" (Anderson et al. 2001). There can be no training without a clear and precise identification of these educational objectives (Goldstein and Ford 2002; Dubiau 2007; Gaultier-Gaillard et al. 2012).

Direct observation throughout the exercise is the most popular method for assessing a group of trainees; however, this must be structured and formalized, and observers also must be trained on how to collect data (Dimock and Kass 2007). Accordingly, observation is a constituent element of assessment (Caird-Daley *et al.* 2007). It is based on the behavior identified by observers: it should ponder the non-technical skills mobilized by a group, that is, group coordination, communication, the leader's ability to direct his group, the decision-making process and the most salient skills every organization should develop (Annett *et al.* 2000; Kosarzycki *et al.* 2002; Gurtner *et al.* 2007). Observation can also help identify whether trainees can mobilize technical skills, such as using specific crisis unit tools: mapping, modeling and information-sharing (Lapierre 2016). Besides, a single observation can detect induced reactions, whether through an event injected into the scenario or through the specific behavior of one of the group members (Fowlkes and Burke 2005). Finally, a team of trainees who solves problems should also be assessed regarding its ability to adapt to the behavior of other members, as well as the cognitive, affective and motivational group resources (Marks *et al.* 2001; Shanahan *et al.* 2007).

However, observation does not suffice, as a method, to evaluate the whole of a training course: observation through behavior is essential, but as a complement to the actions performed by trainees (Salas *et al.* 2009). In other words, it is necessary to combine two types of methodology: one based on the behavioral observation of members and the other related to the accomplishment of the technical aspects of the crisis unit (e.g. decisions and their relevance) (Verdel *et al.* 2010). In summary, this assessment must be conducted both at the individual and the collective level (Salas *et al.* 2009), and as much from a technical point of view as from a non-technical one (Weil *et al.* 2004).

Currently, limitations exist in the observation and assessment of participants during an exercise in crisis management training: these limits concern both the approach and content of the assessment (Goldstein and Ford 2002; Dubiau 2007; Verdel *et al.* 2010). In other words, there is a lack of the formalism of the evaluation as well as of the criteria for carrying it out, particularly in the field of crisis management training.

So, attention was devoted to observation and assessment practices, apart from the crisis training domain, such as the medical, aeronautics, aerospace, military and psychosocial fields. A total of 42 trainee assessment tools were identified, which can be used in three distinct time periods: before, during and after training (Lapierre 2016). In addition to these time periods, different characteristics make it possible to differentiate them: their assessment scale (individual or collective), selected items (assessment or observation criteria), as well as the tool's formalism. Five formal tools include the event checklist (check-boxes with predefined items selected for each major event of the scenario), the grid of behavioral observation (behavior associated with technical and non-technical skills), the semi-virgin grid (which helps the observer in his note-taking during the observation of trainees), the self-assessment questionnaire and the interview (both of which are used to evaluate before or after the exercise).

Special attention should be given to the three types of criteria that are mainly used during the evaluation of a group of trainees:

– the behavioral indicator: this contributes to making real-time observation either at the individual or the group level in their interaction with the environment (Klampfer *et al.* 2001). This approach, initially related to skills, is mainly used to evaluate group processes at work in different situations. It also gives the opportunity to identify "good" and "bad" behavior in connection with the educational objectives (Bahl *et al.* 2010);

– "pre-established" technical expectation: before the exercise, facilitators identify and fill out the tools with technical expectations (actions to be implemented, decisions to be made) all throughout the exercise. These expectations will be checked when detected;

– "free" technical expectation: "expected" empty boxes are available; the observer is expected to identify them in real time and to complete them as the exercise progresses.

The analysis of these different observation criteria makes it possible to detect their matching limitations: on the one hand, since the assessment criteria are mainly focused on behavioral indicators or technical expectations, the evaluation of the group of trainees is partial. Besides, the use of behavioral indicators requires the creation of an educational toolkit from which the latter can be related to pedagogical objectives as well as the required skills for achieving them.

Thus, to address the problem of rating the participants of a crisis management training exercise, it is necessary to build an educational toolkit to be used by facilitators: it is from this element that the assessment tool can be developed. The approach should incorporate several features, such as providing assessment at the crisis unit scale and simultaneously integrate the technical and the non-technical expectations (organizational aspects) of the exercise.

5.3. Methodology

In order to build these assessment tools, a three-step methodology has been proposed (Figure 5.1).

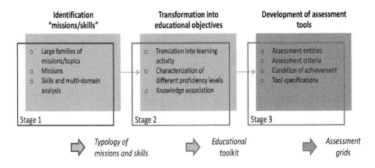

Figure 5.1. *A general methodology for building assessment tools. For a color version of this figure, see www.iste.co.uk/ sauvagnargues/crisis.zip*

The first stage is an essential prerequisite so as to characterize expectations during exercise: it refers to identifying the tasks and skills of a crisis unit. In crisis management-related literature, technical missions have only been mentioned, while organizational missions have been characterized. In total, 17 missions have been identified and grouped in three strategic axes:

– **missions under the strategic crisis response**: specifically related to the hazard, the stakes, the intervention means, the anticipation and the post-crisis;

– **missions specifically related to the crisis unit control** (absent from the literature, except regarding the activation of the crisis unit): management of internal resources, transmission of information, monitoring, the shared vision, coordination, the management of emotions;

– **missions related to crisis communication**: media monitoring, the communication strategy, communication with the general public and the population, with the authorities, communication supported by social networks.

The characterization of these missions was divided into several objectives to accurately determine their achievement modalities. For example, for the mission dedicated to the crisis unit monitoring, five objectives were identified: in fact, the leader's capability to command the unit, to assign tasks and to delegate are at the heart of the procedure and necessary to accomplish the objectives established by the unit. Conflict management and maintaining mutual trust among team members are also distinguished. In total, 64 objectives make it possible to carry out 17 key missions.

The multi-domain analysis of different assessment tools and the psychosocial approaches adopted based on human and organizational factors supplemented by a study on the essential skills for increasing teamwork performance made it possible to identify 15 necessary skills for the members of a crisis unit in the context of major risks. Among these skills, we can particularly mention "proving leadership abilities", "communicating", "promoting a shared vision of the situation", "making decisions", "coordinating", etc. At the end of this first stage, a typology of missions and crisis unit skills was created.

From this mission and objective typology, the aim was to classify the latter into learning activities (in other words, to translate them into educational objectives). In order to enable facilitators to structure their assessment into several levels of difficulty, the educational objectives were built while respecting a hierarchical logic: the three levels were organized around three cognitive sets. The first level of proficiency, or the beginner level, is related to common sense and understanding. The second level of proficiency, or the intermediate level, refers to enforcement and analysis. Finally, the third level of proficiency, or the expert level, is associated with the assessment of the situation.

For example, for the objective of "collecting data related to threatened stakes", at the first level of proficiency, trainees are expected to look for information in documents or in some types of challenge typology in regulatory crisis documents (such as emergency management plans). The expectation for an intermediate level is that trainees should take initiative to refer to a supporting map for collecting data. Finally, the expert proficiency level requires that they contact a crisis actor to check if there is real available evidence regarding the threatened stakes.

At the end of this sequence of classification and construction of learning activities, a total of 192 educational objectives were created (64 objectives × 3 levels = 192 educational objectives). Each of the 15 previously identified skills could be associated with the 192 educational objectives in order to determine which resources must be mobilized to achieve them. The whole of this makes up an educational toolkit that the facilitator can refer to in order to structure his assessment. It is important to observe that during an exercise, the 192 educational objectives are not evaluated at the same time: a selection is made based on the needs of the training exercise.

As part of crisis management simulation exercises, the presence of several facilitators and at least an observer is considered to be systematic: facilitators as well as observers and trainees are able to participate in the assessment. Their joint evaluations may ultimately be useful for assessing the technical and organizational aspects of the crisis unit, its missions as well as the skills used by the participants.

From this educational toolkit, the objective is now to make all of these educational objectives observable and measurable. Indeed, if assessment inevitably involves the characterization of specific educational objectives, it is necessary (1) to allocate the overall educational objectives among the participants and (2) to establish different criteria for making this assessment effective.

It has been observed that the evaluators of a crisis management training exercise fall under three entities: observers, facilitators and trainees:

– **Observers (observation mission)**: physically located in the same room as trainees, they must however be as little intrusive as possible. They observe trainees on what is directly observable, namely group dynamics, leadership in the unit, coordination between members, teamwork, information transmission and sharing, the reactions to an event, the decision-making process and the organization of the crisis unit.

– **Facilitators (assessment mission)**: located in a facilitator room, different from the trainee room, they communicate the different messages from the exercise scenario to trainees through various communication channels. They assess trainees through the answers that the latter provide. Assessment focuses mainly on educational objectives related to results of a technical nature, taking into consideration the construction of the elicited answer, the time frame, the adequacy of the response to the request made by the facilitator, the vocabulary employed, etc. because these elements are difficult to observe in the trainee room. These technical objectives can be assessed by observers in the room when information and decisions are handled by a group.

– **Trainees (self-assessment mission)**: trainees themselves take part in the post-exercise evaluation. This is justified for two reasons: the first is that certain educational objectives cannot be assessed by observers nor by facilitators because they exclusively involve cognitive aspects which are unique to each individual (e.g. "controlling that the daybook is up-to-date and archived"). The second reason is that each learner is also able to self-evaluate, which includes all of the educational objectives that concern them. On the other hand, the analysis of the results of the assessment of trainees after the exercise is not an applicable real-time evaluation technique.

Following this distinction of the assessment entities, the educational toolkit for the association of evaluators was carried out (Table 5.1):

Entities/axis	Strategic crisis response	Strategic crisis organization	Crisis communication
Facilitators	34 educational objectives	6 educational objectives	44 educational objectives
Observers	17 educational objectives	62 educational objectives	15 educational objectives
Trainees	2 educational objectives	10 educational objectives	5 educational objectives

Table 5.1. Distribution of educational objectives according to toolkit evaluators and assessment axes

First of all, the sum of all of these educational objectives is greater than 192 since three objectives are observable, two evaluating entities such as "determining the whole of threatened stakes and mapping them out", which may be evaluated both by facilitators and observers (on the mapping aspect, specifically by the latter).

In the following step, this distribution formalizes the evaluators' assessment, by characterizing the relevant criteria. On the one hand, this formalization requires determining the different evaluation criteria as well as the achievement status of educational objectives. Each of the educational objectives of the toolkit is associated with one or more criterion.

For observers, the latter can rely on a set of behavioral indicators which are built in a generic way, in order to be used regardless of the training exercise. For the first axis of the toolkit ("strategic crisis response"), especially oriented toward technical expectations, criteria are more or less related to the scenario. For the second axis of the toolkit, "strategic crisis organization", criteria are exclusively built on behavioral indicators. Indicators for each objective simultaneously incorporate one or many markers concerning the task to be undertaken and the relationship to the group. Finally, for the last axis ("strategic crisis communication"), criteria are also based on behavioral indicators, but these are related to the organization of the crisis unit in relation to media. For facilitators, the previous method is repeated so as to define the whole of assessment criteria. On the other hand, not being physically located alongside the trainees, all of the assessment criteria regarding them throughout the three axes are technical; that is, they refer to generic expectations related to actions.

The example assessment criteria characterization for the objective "supervising the crisis unit" is chosen here because its three proficiency levels can be evaluated by the observer (Table 5.2). In the following table, "B" corresponds to the educational objectives of the beginner level, "I" to the intermediate level and "E" to the expert level.

Objectives	Educational objectives	Assessment criteria
Axis no. 2 "Carrying out the strategic response"		
Supervising the crisis unit	B: Keeping the crisis unit in a calmed state I: Formulating guidelines to achieve objectives E: Setting the group's operational mode	N: Asking participants to remain quiet/calm, thanks to the leader's attitude I: Providing advice to the group/identifying objectives E: Establishing an operation mode / bearing in mind that decisions must be approved by a supervisor / mentioning the need to fill shared media / designating a referent / the need for communicating the daybook

Table 5.2. *Examples of characterizing the assessment criteria dedicated to observers*

Once the criteria characterization phase is over, it is still essential to set the conditions for achieving each of the 192 educational objectives. The chosen approach is to use the formalism of elementary logical functions (Boolean operations).

In continuity with the previous example, the terms of the educational objectives are as follows:

– For the beginner-level educational objective, "maintaining calm in the crisis unit": in function of the noise in the unit during the exercise, the observer will be able to estimate whether calmness was maintained or not.

– **For the intermediate-level educational objective, "formulating guidelines to achieve objectives"**: "giving advice to the group" and "identifying objectives" that the crisis unit has to achieve are to be observed.

– **Finally, for the expert-level objective, "setting the group's operational mode"**: the leader is expected to establish "an operational mode", meaning that "all decisions must be approved by a supervisor" and that "the daybook" is constantly filled". The use of shared media is also expected: here, it either refers to different members "filling shared media" or to "designating a referent".

The use of elementary logical functions was repeated on the totality of created criteria. Following this stage, all of the elements needed to design assessment tools for observers and facilitators were reunited.

The design of the observation tool revolved around the assumption that the tool for observers should be different from the one destined for facilitators, due to their different physical positions during the simulation exercise. Besides, their respective assessment mission is carried out with different means: the observer has a direct and continuous vision of trainee reactions, while facilitators, depending on the roles that they endorse, only have telephone, fax or email interactions.

The organization of these two tools revolves around four structural points: the use time period, the evaluation scale, the assessment support and the contents (Table 5.3).

Tool structuring	For the observer tool	For the facilitator tool
Use time period	Real time, per phase	Real time, per phase
Evaluation scale	Collective and individual	Collective and individual
Assessment support	Event checklist and behavioral grid	Event checklist via control messages and specific checklist
Contents	Behavioral indicators and technical expectations (major orientation)	Technical expectations, employed vocabulary, "actor/request" consistency

Table 5.3. *Structural choices of assessment tools for the use of observers and facilitators*

Regarding these two tools, it is important to observe that the exercise scenario is broken down into different phases by evaluators. This breakdown, transparent to trainees, corresponds to the occurrence of major events involved in the scenario. Thus, facilitators and observers can better understand the reactions of trainees based on a potentially disruptive event at the crisis unit.

As regards observers, the observation tool thus created combines two approaches: that of the event checklist (in which educational expectations may vary according to the different phases of the scenario) and the behavioral approach. The use of behavioral indicators is preferred by observers. As regards facilitators, they can also evaluate educational expectations according to the different phases of the scenario: the creation of scenario control messages injected throughout the exercise makes it possible to verify a certain number of expectations, while specific checklists are created simultaneously (for assessing the contents of a situational review, for example).

Finally, the evaluation jointly conducted by observers and facilitators has been designed to be dynamic and interactive:

– **It is dynamic** because different educational objectives are distributed between observers and facilitators based on their assessment ability, and also because educational objectives are evaluated according to the different phases of the scenario.

– **It is interactive** because it is based on the achievement of trainee educational objectives throughout the exercise, at the time that new requests can be injected into the scenario. This feature is made possible through communication between observers and facilitators during the exercise and also due to the creation of a list of predefined requests to be injected into the scenario in case different educational objectives are not met throughout the exercise.

A typology of requests was thus created to (indirectly and unobtrusively) encourage trainees to meet the previously set objectives. For example, if the observer finds that there is no prioritization of the objectives to be achieved, or that there is no situational review, etc., they can send a notification to the master facilitator so as to inject a message from a hierarchical superior or authority asking for a structured and complete review of the situation.

5.4. Results

This evaluation methodology, named EVADE (EValuation and Assistance for DEbriefing), was developed through an iterative approach through observation conducted on almost 39 exercises. The results presented in this section come from a simulation exercise organized by the IMT Mines Ales crisis management platform. Trainees taking part in this exercise were students, and the chosen level of proficiency was "neophyte". Five facilitators and two observers were also present during the one hour and 45 minutes that the exercise lasted. An accident of dangerous material took place in a neighborhood of a medium-sized town with sensitive stakes (school, retirement home, place of worship, homes, shops) which required the activation of the communal crisis unit. The scenario writer sequenced the script in three major observation phases, with a focus first on the management of the TDG accident (generating a cabin fire and a toxic rejection), second, on the protection of stakes as a result of the build-up of a toxic cloud and, finally, on the last phase, regarding the management of a new major event, the starting of a forest fire.

From the very first moments of the exercise, two observers assessed the crises-related educational objectives and formulated the preliminary guidelines. In the educational toolkit, this corresponds to objectives entitled "introducing oneself at a crisis unit", "carrying out the preliminary actions", "supervising the crisis unit" and "orienting the crisis unit". For the rest of the exercise, a first observer paid special attention to leadership in action in the unit, particularly assessing the following objectives: "orienting the crisis unit", "distributing and delegating the group's tasks", "deploying authority skills" and "reviewing the situation". The second observer focused on the overall coordination between members and the sharing of information, while assessing the following objectives: "managing information transmission", "exchanging information", "coordinating the sub-units" and "making decisions as a group".

For each of the abovementioned objectives, the observer built their grid with all of the corresponding assessment criteria. For example, the assessment objective "orienting the crisis unit" appeared in the grid in the following manner (Figure 5.2):

SUPERVISING THE CRISIS UNIT		Yes	No	Observations
9.1	**Introducing the objectives to be collectively achieved**			
WHO	Through DOS			
	By means of another sub-unit			
WHAT	Phenomenon-related objectives			
	Objectives related to target/action preservation			
9.1	**Communicating the priorities to be achieved**			
WHO	Through DOS			
	By means of another sub-unit			
WHAT	Refreshing objectives			
	Phenomenon-related priorities			
ON	Priorities related to stake/action preservation			
9.1	**The use and control of existing procedures**			
	Requesting the use of CSP procedures			
	Controlling their use			

Figure 5.2. *An example of the objective assessment "directing the crisis unit" by observer no. 1. For a color version of this figure, see www.iste.co.uk/sauvagnargues/crisis.zip*

The observation grid of observer no. 1 was organized in such a way as to harmonize with the other three objectives concerning this observer.

Then, the five facilitators of the exercise simultaneously played several roles. For example, facilitator no. 3 played two roles, that of the Municipal Police and that of the media. In the light of the estimated level of proficiency of trainees, it was decided that three objectives would be assessed for each of them:

– **For the "Municipal Police" role**: the assessment objectives were "determining closed roads", "managing the preservation actions of threatened stakes" and "identifying available resources".

– **For the "media" role**: the assessment objectives were "transmitting instructions", "communicating a consistent message" and "following the given instructions". The latter refers to the fact that the crisis unit may wish to contact only one correspondent per media, to set its own conditions for interacting with them and honoring their commitments (appointment times and meeting points, for example).

As for the objectives assessed by observers, facilitators assess their objectives using different evaluation criteria, as featured in the educational toolkit. The formalism of the tool is in line with that of the observers.

After filling out the tools during the exercise, these two assessment entities, observers and facilitators, establish the trends indicated by the different objectives they evaluated. For example, the observer who focused on the first directions given by the leader in the unit recorded all of his comments in the assessment tool (Figure 5.3).

PRELIMINARY ORIENTATIONS OF THE UNIT		Yes	No	Observations
9.1	**Introducing the objectives to be collectively achieved**			
WHO	Through DOS		X	
	By means of another sub-unit		X	
WHAT	Phenomenon-related objectives		X	
	Objectives related to stake/action preservation		X	
9.2	**Distributing tasks to the unit**			
WHO	Through DOS	X		
	By means of another sub-unit	X		No distribution but questioning
WHAT	To a sub-unit		X	
	To all the sub-units	X		Is there a school, a hospital, targets in the area?
9.1	**Communicating the priorities to be achieved**			
WHO	Through DOS		X	
	By means of another sub-unit		X	
WHAT	Refreshing objectives		X	
	Phenomenon-related priorities		X	
ON	Priorities related to stake/action preservation			
9.1	**The use and control of existing procedures**			
	Requesting the use of CSP procedures	X		The leader addresses their sub-units
	Controlling their use		X	

Figure 5.3. *Observation data concerning the leader's preliminary directions to the crisis unit. For a color version of this figure, see www.iste.co.uk/sauvagnargues/crisis.zip*

The observer noticed that at the beginning, the leader did not properly introduce the objectives which had to be collectively achieved. On the other hand, the leader succeeded in attempting an early division of labor, especially regarding the active search for potential stakes in the area affected by the toxic cloud. However, the observer's notes reflected that this division of tasks was not made in a clear and explicit manner, as they later asked the whole group. Next, no intermediate-level criterion was checked concerning a possible prioritization of tasks to be performed, be it related to the phenomenon, to the stakes involved or to protective actions. Finally, and this is important to observe, one expected expert level was observed: to encourage members of the unit to use the emergency procedures from the available emergency management plan.

The facilitators also obtained data related to the various objectives assessed throughout the exercise. If we pick up the example of one of the objectives assessed by the facilitator simulating the Municipal Police, the latter can show that the crisis unit was quite competitive on the issue of closed roads: the two neophyte-level expectations were achieved as well as four criteria in five from the intermediate level (Figure 5.4).

		Yes	Time	Details of collected answers
3.1	**Asking for the implementation of road closures as regards the toxic cloud**			
REQUEST	Request was addressed at my sub-unit	X	10h14	
	Request for the establishment of closed roads	X	10h14	Request the closure of 100 m, but no barriers
3.1	**Justifying the choice of closed roads**			
ZONE	Communicating the size of the perimeter	X	10h14	
CLOSED ROADS	"La montée des Lauriers" roundabout	X	10h19	Road intersection of Royale St and Sorbier St
	Cauvel Quay and Léo Lagrange St			
	Royale St roundabout (to the north)	X	10h19	This is precisely what was requested
JUSTIFICATION	Because of the ongoing phenomenon	X	10h19	
3.1	**To control the holding of closed roads and readapt them in relation to the fire**			
READAPT	Chemin de Montaud			
	Cauvel Quay, at the intersection with Churchill bridge			
	Montée des Lauriers			
INSTRUCTIONS	Make room for the firefighters to move			
	Ask for a confirmation of action taken	X	10h24	Request a confirmation of the arrival of barriers
	Report road closure to the Manager			

Figure 5.4. *Assessment data concerning the management of closed roads. For a color version of this figure, see www.iste.co.uk/sauvagnargues/crisis.zip*

Thus, at the end of the exercise, facilitators and observers had different elements to help them with their feedback during the debriefing phase. Nevertheless, it is important to remember that the objective is not to present quantitative data during debriefing, nor to address the objectives one by one from a perspective of success or failure. The idea is rather to obtain a set of technical and organizational results concerning the different phases of the exercise. Finally, as skills are also associated with different educational objectives, observers can also opt for an approach to visualize which skills were mobilized during the exercise, rather than the achievement (or not) of the pre-established educational objectives (Lapierre *et al.* 2016).

5.5. Conclusion

In view of all of the deficiencies found in crisis units during the occurrence of major events, the training of crisis decision-makers becomes a necessity. The proposal of a structured methodology to observe and evaluate the participants of an exercise is also essential in view of current methodological limitations and practices. The EVADE method, based on assessment tools already used in other risk areas, offers an innovative tool for facilitators. In the context of a crisis management simulation exercise, while integrating technical and organizational expectations, the totality of the suggested assessment tools relies on the creation of an educational toolkit, divided into 17 missions, 64 objectives and 192 educational objectives, as well as its accompanying assessment criteria. The latter enables facilitators to work on the missions of a crisis unit and the skills of its members, thanks to the 192 learning activities and their associated assessment criteria. In addition to these elements, another EVADE objective is to guide facilitators and observers in their assessment both during the exercise (formalizing it) and the debriefing phase. Nowadays, the prospects for improvement are particularly aimed at optimizing the development of the observation and evaluation tools. An effort should also be made regarding data processing from these tools, because these are highly significant as a result of the exercises. Currently, an improvement of these tools is under way, and a debriefing support tool is being designed.

5.6. References

Anderson, L.W., Krathwohl, D.R., Airasian, P., Cruikshank, K., Mayer, R., Pintrich, P., Raths, J., and Wittrock, M. (2001). *A Taxonomy for Learning, Teaching and Assessing: A Revision of Bloom's Taxonomy.* Longman Publisher, New York.

Annett, J., Cunningham, D., and Mathias-Jones, P. (2000). A method for measuring team skills. *Ergonomics*, 43, 1076–1094.

Bahl, R., Murphy, D.J., and Strachan, B. (2010). Non-technical skills for obstetricians conducting forceps and vacuum deliveries: Qualitative analysis by interviews and video recordings. *Eur. J. Obstet. Gynecol. Reprod. Biol.*, 150, 147–151.

Beaubien, J. and Baker, D. (2004). The use of simulation for training teamwork skills in health care: How low can you go? *Qual. Saf. Health Care*, 13, i51–i56.

Caird-Daley, A.K., Harris, D., Bessell, K., and Lowe, M. (2007). Training decision-making using serious games. Report, Human Factors Integration Defense Technology Centre. HFIDTC/2/WP4 6.

Crocq, L., Huberson, S., and Vraie, B. (2009). *Gérer les grandes crises sanitaires, économiques, politiques et économiques.* Odile Jacob.

Dautun, C. (2007). Contribution à l'étude des crises de grande ampleur : connaissance et aide à la décision pour la Sécurité Civile. Thesis, Ecole Nationale Supérieure des Mines de Saint-Etienne.

Dautun, C. and Lacroix, B. (2013). Crise et décision : plongée au coeur des cellules de crise. *Cahiers de la Sécurité et de la justice*, 24.

Dimock, H.G. and Kass, R.R. (2007). *How to Observe Your Group.* Captus Press, Canada.

Dubiau, P. (2007). Gestion d'une urgence radiologique : Organisation et fonctionnement. *Techniques l'ingénieur*, Génie nucléaire, BN3870.

Fowlkes, J.E. and Burke, S.C. (2005). Event-based approach to training (EBAT). In *Handbook of Human Factors and Ergonomic Methods*, Stanton, N., Hedge, A., Bookhuis, K., Salas, E., and Hendrick H. (eds). CRC Press, Boca Raton.

Fowlkes, J.E., Dwyer, D.J., Oser, R.L., and Salas, E. (1998). Event-based approach to training (EBAT). *Int. J. Aviat. Psychol.*, 8(3), 209–221.

Gaba, D.M. (2004). The future vision of simulation in health care. *Qual. Saf. Health Care*, 13(1), i2–i10.

Gaultier-Gaillard, S., Persin, M., and Vraie, B. (2012). Gestion de crise – Les exercices de simulation : de l'apprentissage à l'alerte, La Plaine.

Goldstein, I.L. and Ford, J.K. (2002). *Training in organizations: needs, assessment, development, and evaluation*, 4th edition. Wadsworth Thomson Learning, Belmont.

Gurtner, A., Tschan, F., Semmer, N.K., and Nägele, C. (2007). Getting groups to develop good strategies: Effects of reflexivity interventions on team process, team performance, and shared mental models. *Organizational Behavior and Human Decision Processes*, 102(2), 127–142.

Heiderich, D. (2010). *Plan de gestion de crise*. Dunod.

Klampfer, B., Flin, R., Helmreich, R., Häusler, R., Sexton, B., Fletcher, G., Field, P., Staender, S., Lauche, K., Dieckmann, P., and Amacher, A. (2001). Behavioural markers workshop – group interaction in high risk environments. *Enhancing Perform. High Risk Environ. Recomm. Use Behav. Markers*, 6–33.

Kosarzycki, M.P., Salas, E., Wilson, K.A., and DeRouin, R. (2002). Teamwork training in organizations: The case of training resource management. *Psykhe Rev. la Esc. Psicol.*, 11, 121–140.

Lachtar, D. (2012). Contribution des systèmes multi-agent à l'analyse de la performance organisationnelle d'une cellule de crise communale. Thesis, Ecole Nationale Supérieure des Mines de Paris.

Lagadec, P. (2012). *Du risque majeur aux mégachocs*. Préventique.

Lapierre, D. (2016). Méthode EVADE : une approche intégrée pour l'EValuation et l'Aide au DEbriefing. Thesis, University of Nîmes.

Lapierre, D., Tixier, J., Tena-Chollet, F., Bony-Dandrieux, A., and Weiss, K. (2016). Developing an EVADE (EVAluation and DEbriefing) method to assess trainees during crisis management training for major hazards and feedback them. *Chem. Eng. Trans.*, 48, 877–882.

Maisonneuve, D. (2010). *Les relations publiques dans une société en mouvance*, 4th edition. PUQ, Sainte-Foy.

Marks, M.A., Mathieu, J.E., and Zaccaro, S.J. (2001). A temporally based framework and taxonomy of team processes. *Acad. Manag. Rev.*, 26, 356–376.

Power, D., Henn, P., Power, T., and McAdoo, J. (2013). An evaluation of high fidelity simulation training for paramedics in Ireland. *Int. Paramed. Pract.*, 2, 11–18.

Ramspacher, M.-S. (2013). L'évaluation de la formation, une préoccupation secondaire. *Lestchos*.

Raybourn, E.M. (2005). Adaptive thinking & leadership training for cultural awareness and communication competence. *Interact. Technol. Smart Educ.*, 2, 127–130.

Salas, E. and Cannon-Bowers, J. (1997). Methods, tools and strategies for team training. In *Training for a Rapidly Changing Workplace: Applications of Psychogical Research*, Quiñones, M.A., Ehrenstein, A. (eds). Washington, DC.

Salas, E., Rosen, M.A., Held, J.D., and Weissmuller, J.J. (2009). Performance measurement in simulation-based training: A review and best practices. *Simul. Gaming*, 40, 328–376.

Sayegh, L., Anthony, W.P., and Perrew, P.L. (2004). Managerial decision-making under crisis: The role of emotion in an intuitive decision process. *Hum. Resour. Manag. Rev.*, 14, 179–199.

Shanahan, C., Best, C., Finch, M., and Sutton, C. (2007). Measurement of the behavioural, cognitive, and motivational factors underlying team performance. Report, Australian Department of Defence, Defence Science and Technology Organisation (DSTO), Fishermans Bend.

Verdel, T., Tardy, A., Lopez, P., Hansen, C., and Deschanels, J. (2010). iCrisis[TM]: Un dispositif original de simulation de gestion de crise.

Weil, S.A., Hussain, T.S., Diedrich, F.J., Ferguson, W., and Macmillan, J. (2004). Assessing distributed team performance in DARWARS training: Challenges and methods. *Proceedings of the Interservice/Industry Training, Simulation, and Education Conference, 17ème Congrès de Maîtrise des Risques et de Sûreté de Fonctionnement*, Orlando, 1–10.

Managing the Game
Within Crisis Exercises

6.1. Introduction

Crisis exercises are known to teach good practices for real situations, revealing the weaknesses of an organization facing the crisis or increasing the awareness of a possible crisis.

By primarily focusing the design and analysis of these exercises on a rational appraisal *ex post facto*, the essence of what happens during such a simulation is often lost: for example, the interactions between the players and their partnership, the varying levels of understanding of the situations, individual and collective strategies, risks and decisions made, the enjoyment of achieving some objectives and the disappointment from missed ones. We call this evanescent state "playful dynamics" or "Ludicity" (from *ludus*, not to be confused with lucidity), which strongly binds players in the same liminal space but disappears as soon as the simulation ceases.

In this chapter, we are interested in the playful dynamics at work when a group of trainees agrees to seriously consider for a few hours that they will live a virtual crisis situation together, and especially in (1) the key components of Lucidity, (2) the manifestations of Ludicity and (3) how to manage the Ludicity. To this end, we draw on the

Chapter written by David GOUTX, Sophie SAUVAGNARGUES and Laurent MERMET.

lessons learned from analyses of playful simulation, as well as the reflections of live action role-playing game players on their practices.

The bias used for this chapter is to consider the crisis exercise played in a simulation room as a game.

Indeed, crisis exercises are a good tool for learning best practices, tested in real situations, to come face to face with the limitations of an organization dealing with a crisis, or to experience a crisis virtually and realize how weighty it is (Boin *et al.* 2004; Smith 2004; Carenzo *et al.* 2016). Transforming the lessons of simulations into a real-life competence requires a rigorously structured exercise: defining the learning objectives, creating the simulation to achieve them and debriefing the simulation with observations guided by proper analytical tools.

6.1.1. *The concept of Ludicity: a definition*

People's interest in games is not new. It has given rise to theoretical and practical advances which can be put into two main categories: serious games and gamification.

A serious game is a game designed to teach, using serious, professional elements, in a playful environment so as to promote their learning by the player. It could be a virtual simulator reproducing more or less exactly a professional activity in order for the player to be in a situation as close to reality as possible, or it could be a game created to model the intricacies of a given profession/professional activity (Floodranger, Comod), or even classic games revamped with professional elements (happy families card game with a risk prevention slant). The trainee is perfectly aware that they are playing a game and that by playing the game they are acquiring a competence.

Gamification is based on interlacing playful elements into a serious activity or a professional environment in order to increase the involvement of the targeted person in his task. In its simplest aspect, it involves giving points, creating scores and making them known to the person to encourage him to maximize these scores by prioritizing the highest value activities, or even generating competition – with other people engaged in the same activity. These types of games are more to do with increasing the person involvement in the activity than increasing a competence. The person is not really conscious that they are playing a game but is aware that their activity is modified by the addition of these game elements.

What we are looking at in this chapter is neither the serious game nor gamification, but rather we are looking to identify what in a given activity, here the management of a simulated crisis, relates to a game mechanism or what part of the activity is play. Thus, once these game elements are identified, they can be used to guide the creation and management of this activity, to increase or reduce the play part depending on the desired result but without changing the nature of the task/activity. The person is not really conscious that they are playing a game but they are more or less consciously activating their inner player. This still less well-known approach has been conceptualized under the name *jouabilité* (Henriot 1989) or framification (Lieberoth 2014). It is to a game what storytelling is to communication: a way to organize elements which are not inherently playful into a playful system without allowing the person to be engaged in the known activity.

For a long time, play has been thought of as purely a child's domain (and it was thus studied by Wittgenstein or Piaget, for example), as opposed to the supposedly serious nature of adult activities. However, game theorists (Huizinga 1938; Caillois 1953; Henriot 1989; Suits 2014) have gradually reduced this opposition and shown the power of the concept of gameplay which can be understood as the theory of imaginary action or of the imagination in action. Finally, gameplay is less to be opposed to seriousness but more to the virtual: it enables us to materialize one of the infinite numbers of possibilities springing from our imagination through the medium of play.

In effect, a crisis management exercise entails putting 6–10 players in a crisis management room to act as the key figures in a crisis committee and to make them deal with a crisis scenario developed by the training team. This is done by making them play their roles and interact between themselves and with external actors in the crisis played by the training team. This description could put in mind a role-playing game; however, the absence of any game master facing the players and the fact that the players are living their actions rather than simply describing them more gives the feeling of a live action role-playing game (Hitchens and Drachen 2009).

There is no doubt that these exercises are potential games. As soon as the aim is to immerse yourself in a virtual situation, by acting as if there was a real crisis to manage, one is by nature (and not intent) in a play-situation. A lot will depend on the level of freedom the person in charge of the exercise leaves to the participant to immerse themselves in the playfulness of the situation.

6.2. Key components of Ludicity

6.2.1. *The span of the game space*

The game is first characterized by the creation of an imaginary space where the game takes place, in which the players get together and agree to suspend reality.

This imaginary space is sometimes called liminal space (with reference to the work of Van Gennep on rituals), sometimes diegetic space (with reference to the work of Harviainen and Lieberoth (2012) on role-playing games). This liminal space exists as soon as at least two players agree to consider certain real objects, actions or persons as being part of the game space if the players give them a defined meaning in their imaginary space. For example, such and such a room within the "Ecole des Mines d'Ales" will be considered as a crisis management room, and this or that printer will be considered to be a fax machine in direct contact with the "Prefecture".

The creation of a game space consists of pooling the imagination of all the players, focused on a common interpretation of a fictional situation (Waskul and Lust 2004).

The first problem that arises when the players' imagination is strongly activated, with little or no visual aids, is how close each player's interpretation of the fictional situation is to the reality.

Each player builds his own understanding of the situation; nothing guarantees that this understanding is close enough to the fictional situation of the exercise or even close to the understanding of another player. This difficulty grows exponentially with each player being added to the same simulation. Only the sharing of each player's understanding of the situation can highlight such a dissonance, if it is there, and remedy it.

Beyond the understanding of the situation, the involvement of each player in this game space is also part of the game space. The second problem is thus to keep all the players together in the same game space. It is possible that as the game progresses, the initial group becomes two or more sub-groups of players, each with their own logic solidly anchored to the initial game space but multiplying sub-spaces in the game, all existing at the same time. There again, only the sharing of each group's diverging interpretation of the same element of the game can enable the players to recognize this divergence through a dissonance (called "the emperor's new clothes dissonance" by McGonigal as inspired by Andersen's tale).

These dissonances are thus inherently part of the development of the game space, both a moment of vulnerability and of reinforcement of the game. A vulnerability is when the players confront the interpretations they have of the situation where not all of them will be right. Some will have to accept the new representation of the situation, resulting from the dissonance they just navigated through. However, if they are invested, motivated or got used to their representation of the situation, it is very likely that they will lose their motivation or engagement with the new representation created by the dissonance. At worst, a dissonance can lead some players to purely and simply leave the diegetic space. However, once the dissonance is out of the way, a reinforcement may occur, which makes the whole group of players come back with the same interpretation of the situation. Realizing the extent of this new collective representation gives each player an opportunity to think his actions through and be more efficient in this newly extended strategic depth.

All the payers do not have the same role when facing the dissonance. In fact, the dissonance is not usually resolved through the majority rule. At least one player is invested by the other players, sometimes in spite of themself, and often without anybody realizing it, with some kind of cognitive authority (as defined by Van Gennep (1909) in his study of rituals). Whether this is right or wrong is of no importance to the fact that the players trust that player to define the truth in their diegetic space. This can be linked to the part played by this player, their ease in playing the game and the level of competence attributed to the player in real life: all eyes are on them, and all listen to them when they define right and wrong in the game space (Goutx 2014).

The way in which this player acknowledges, more or less consciously, this role of cognitive authority is a significant factor in determining how the group of players will act in the game space. If their interpretations and decisions are contrary to the ideas of the training team, they can lose all control over the game.

6.2.2. Magic circle and rabbit hole

The players immersed in their diegetic space are still conscious of the rest of their environment, but the attention they give it is dependent on their degree of involvement in the game space. In other words, they can become so engrossed by the game that they are partially blind and deaf to the evolution of their environment. This shaping of a space in which the player retires from the outside world has been called the "Magic Circle" since Huizinga (1938), without always fully representing all the subtleties of this concept. It is not a rigid border separating game and reality but much more a collective resistance of the players to allowing elements from outside the game space to intrude on it (Harviainen 2012).

Concerning the crisis management exercise, being an immersive game and even a pervasive one (as called by McGonigal, 2003) with a starting point that the player's environment is the game environment, there will always be some porosity between the diegetic or liminal space and the player's environment. The ability of the players to discern which elements of their environment should have a place in their diegetic space is very reliant on a kind of pre-coding of these elements according to the specific rules of the game space. Thus, one player telling any given information to the others out loud is not enough for the other players to acknowledge and internalize it. They need to see the characteristics of these external elements that will integrate these information in the game space.

Information that is certified by players taking on the mantle of cognitive authority in the exercise is immediately part of the diegetic space. It is not only the defining characteristic of the cognitive authority but also what makes a player a cognitive authority. More or less consciously, players have a tendency to offer information to those who took on the mantle of cognitive authority, like they would an offering to the master of a ritual. However, information brought by other players can also become part of the diegetic space immediately if they have characteristics that show they obviously belong to the diegetic space.

Some words linked to the context of the game are like passwords for any information. Thus, the same information given in a factual manner ("I just received a call from the Swiss consul's wife, her daughter is in labor") or in a manner geared toward the diegetic space (potential diplomatic crisis: the daughter of the Swiss consul is in labor and needs urgent medical help) will become part of the game space or not.

All objects in the players' environment are subject to this same selection of what gets into the game space and what stays outside. For example, it is clear for the training team in charge of the crisis management exercise that the printer in this simulated crisis room is a fax machine through which all the information on the crisis from the other organizations managing the crisis with the players will arrive. Although this information has been given to the players at the beginning of the simulation, they will consider this printer as a fax machine that they need to keep an eye on only after they accept the first printout from it as part of the game.

Another prime example is what happens to mobile phones during the simulation. They are generally forbidden during the crisis management exercise, in order to not allow external pressures (phone calls, e-mails, SMS) to take the players out of the diegetic space. This banning of the mobile phone from the start of the simulation pushes it out of the game space: whatever happens during the game, the use of a mobile phone by a player will not be considered by the others as part of the simulation. However, a significant part of the communications during a crisis is done via mobile phones (at least as long as mobile networks are up). Therefore, a player dealing with the intrusion of calls, external to the crisis management exercise, could be considered as part of what this person would have to do in a real crisis. Finally, this instruction could be misunderstood by the players, as they are summoned to the crisis management center by an SMS from the training team to reflect how it would happen in a real crisis. The mobile phone thus assumes the function of a rabbit hole (according to McGonigal, in reference to the rabbit hole into which Alice goes down to reach Wonderland), which gives access to the game space, but afterwards is put out of the game space by the training team's choice.

It is important to note that voluntarily exiting the game space is not such a threat to the whole of the diegetic space. One or more players can decide to temporarily leave the game (often called "game out") to talk between players rather than between characters, to share their understanding of the game situation or even to deal with personal needs not related to the game (have a coffee, make a personal call).

6.2.3. *Characters and persona*

If it is common to distinguish between the real situation and the fictional one when talking about crisis management exercises, we have to acknowledge that the distinction between the player and his character is rarely thought of. The first is the real person that takes part in the exercise, and the second is the projection of that person in a role played in this fictional situation (Waskul and Lust 2004).

However, one only has to consider that the exercise is played in a simulator, a space that the players are not familiar with but asked to consider at the crisis management center although they are more than likely familiar with the actual crisis management center they are supposed to use in a real crisis, to understand that the players have to imagine themselves in roles similar (but not identical) to the ones they would have in a real crisis. It is even possible to say that if the players are not familiar with a real crisis nor its scope or how to deal with it, they will have to create a role for themselves without the help of a real example.

In any case, the fact that the player acts himself as a person in the fictional situation of the crisis management exercise should not hide the fictional doppelgänger whose skin he gets into, to be able to interact with the simulation. This doppelgänger is, in a way, his vehicle through the simulation, the more sophisticated for the richness and sophistication of the role: for example, a role as a recording secretary is less complex than that as a director of emergency operations.

The efficiency of the relationship between a player and his character is dependent on the participant's playing ability (Kapp 2013). This ability is based both on a form of game culture (although it is shown in the literature that this culture brings only a barely detectable and marginal advantage to the one that has it compared to the one that has not acquired it) and how well the player learned the normal ways to act and levers of the simulation. A player can learn this from two main sources. First, they can learn on their own through using the game material available (character's sheet or role sheet). Second, they can imitate another player who seems more at ease, or they can just ask for advice on how to behave (Tychsen *et al.* 2007). This learning curve will automatically create a lag at the beginning of the simulation while the players are not fully efficient in their roles.

In a subtler way, the interaction between a player and their character might be complicated by the fact that the player does not (purposefully or otherwise) exactly play their own role in the simulation, or that the role as defined by the training team is different from the experience and understanding the player has of it. The player then has to deal differently from what they know as a real person with what their character knows. It is even more important if the person has prior knowledge of some content of the exercise that would enable them to anticipate or accelerate the actions of their character in the simulation, thus potentially damaging the realism of the simulation and creating a dissonance. In other words, the competence in gameplay is not necessarily the ability to outfox the scenario but the ability to allow it to develop in a realistic manner and to properly interact with it.

Another potential interaction between the player and their character is any knowledge the character was not supposed to have that the player has, and that can be thus transferred from the player to the character. So, if the player knows that, in real life, within the fictional circumstances they are in, they would have access to resources they are aware of (pool of retirees ready to re-up, any other network they can activate, etc.), they can push their character to demand they are made use of in the game. Thus, the player inserts something that was not there in the game: the efficient use of this freedom (due to the playful nature of the exercise) requires the training team to allow its use and for the cognitive authority in control of the "Magic Circle" to approve of it.

6.2.4. *Game master*

All games rely on a framework of rules that all the players adhere to. The simplest games have one or a few rules, easy enough to understand so that the players will understand them, respect them and make one another respect them. As soon as the complexity increases, either because the rules are opened to interpretation (e.g. make sure your actions are realistic) or because some of the elements of the game are highly changeable and thus the players need to regularly update their individual and collective understandings of these elements, the game needs a game master.

Among the usual duties of the game master (deciding between conflicting interpretations, narrating the story and providing contextual elements to the players, acting as non-player characters, that is, characters not played by one of the players but with which the players nonetheless will interact), some are discharged in the liminal space (then called game-in) and some in the real environment (then called game-out).

The training team, which prepares, organizes and then orchestrates the various components of the game, is instinctively perceived as fulfilling the game master's role. This supposes that the game develops in a unique game space: as soon as it fractures into several liminal sub-spaces, the training team might lose control over part of the game, and then the game master's role for one or more of these sub-spaces might devolve to the cognitive authority who maintains the coherence of that sub-space.

The risk to the proper flow of the game is then a conflict between the training team and its rival in this seceding liminal sub-space: by the nature of the cognitive authority, the players involved are more than likely to follow this authority rather than the elements given by the training team; then, the only way for the training team to recover their authority is to have a game-out adjustment, but that runs the risk of destroying some of the diegesis the players were adhering to.

Although this does not necessarily compromise the good flow of the game, the training team must adapt to this extra dimension and modify the way it is leading the game if they are even aware of this extra dimension.

6.3. Manifestations of Ludicity

6.3.1. *Engagement and pedagogy*

Pedagogues are so interested in games because it has been proven for a while that what is learned through play is acquired faster and better than in the absence of play (Lantis 1998; Sussking and Corburn 1999; Gredler 2004; Daniau 2005; Hopeametsä 2008; Szilas *et al.* 2009; Von Schaik 2012; Chowanda *et al.* 2016; Stavroulia *et al.* 2016). One of the reasons for this is that the trainee is active in the process of learning rather than being passive.

The engagement of the player with the game is more complex than meets the eye: the player loses themself to some extent (which is called the degree of engagement) in the game and its rules while still being aware that it is only a game and they can step out of it at any time.

As for Ludicity in crisis management exercises, which pushes the participants in a game to some extent despite themselves, the engagement is of a similar nature. The fact that participants step into the role attributed to them and accept the hierarchical structure between the characters of the team in the simulation with more or less good grace is the participants' entry point in the ludic space of the exercise. These elements imposed at the start of the exercise last despite creating tensions during the exercise, with one participant accepting more or less graciously, as a person, that playing their character means submitting to another's authority, and another participant accepting to stay within the limits of their role without grabbing the competences attributed to another participant's character. This fact shows not only the conscious willingness of the players to play the game despite the tensions it generates but also a reluctance (not as obvious to them) to be the one player that would endanger the game by stepping out of it.

Measuring the engagement of players in order to maximize it and its effects on the efficiency of the participant's learning is not only a prolific field of study but also very much guided by the work on "Flow", as conceptualized by Csíkszentmihályi (Csíkszentmihályi 1990; Nakamura and Csíkszentmihályi 2002). It is difficult to measure a player's engagement, that fluctuates during the game (Shernoff 2014), without disrupting it by the intrusion of the observation apparatus. This measurement is essentially hindered in this instance by restricting its scope to only ludic activities that lead to high achievement. In the case of crisis management exercises, a player's engagement is due less to an assumed competition for the best crisis manager or a search for the ideal resolution of the crisis, but more to an honest and courageous engagement of the players with crisis situations which, by their very nature, will test the limits of their capacity to act and react.

More specifically, the participants' engagement in a crisis management exercise shows that they feel involved in the fictional situation they are steeped into, play their roles to the best of their abilities, allow others do the same and, if possible, contribute positively to solving the problems happening one after another (or all at once) during this exercise.

The parallel between role-playing games (table game or live action) is very enlightening: the best memories from games are often those associated with strong emotions felt individually or collectively during a certain moment in the game. It is then easy to speak about a state of grace, which is linked to role-playing and simply to the shared pleasure of playing together. While this feeling that is quite obvious to whoever felt it during a game is not well documented, it is enough for the moment to understand that it is linked to emotions felt by the player and other players of his team. Rather than trying to maximize a "Flow" that does not seem fit to describe the participants' engagement in a crisis management exercise, it would be more useful to help create emotions which will by their repetition, intensity and diversity, anchor the game situation in the memory of the player and with it, the learning the training team wishes the players to retain.

6.3.2. *Style of play*

There are many modes of engagement with the game that the players can mobilize and combine to create their own unique style of playing (Morissette 2010).

Thus, by adopting an egotistical mode of engagement, the players will aim to the best of their abilities to resolve the crisis situation, which they are in charge of, by focusing on an individual approach even if it means an appearance of performance rather than an effective performance. For example, when a player understands that the member of the training team who is in charge of providing all the information from the outside world is their main source of solicitation, then they can try to pressurize this trainer to provide more information from the outside world to the point of taking so much of the trainer's time that they will not be able to push the player. This style of play is really gaming the system, exploiting a deficiency in the game rules to shine in the game without deserving it (Franck 2012). Such a behavior, which might steam from a wrong understanding of the aims of the simulation or from the fear of being judged by the other players, does not have a major impact on the simulation: it simply deprives the group of players of the input of the player who immured himself in this egotistical style of play and paralyzes the member of the training team.

The assumptions used to create a crisis management scenario seem to be conducive to a more theatrical style of play for the players, that is, imitating what one thinks is the role to be played. However, very little of a theatrical style is evidenced by the players: most of the interactions are done in a neutral tone and display some kind of reserve on their part. It is even rare for the players to call one another by their names, who instead labor to establish some communication from afar within the room and wait until they are close to one another or look at one another before interacting. The situation evolves when the tension rises, whether due to annoyance against a player in the room, against the problems coming from the training team making the scenario progress or by the player imitating the theatrical style usually adopted by the trainers in order to flesh out the non-player characters that they inhabit at that time. The instructions are then given in a more abrupt tone; the style used to convince the non-player characters played by the trainers becomes more florid. Paradoxically, adopting this theatrical style also brings a certain dose of improvisation which might bring realistic elements into the game space that the training team had not planned to incorporate in the exercise. The tendency is usually for the training team to discourage this theatrical style for this very reason. However, once a player has tasted the theatrical dimension of their role, and realized not only how efficient it is in the exercise but also how much pleasure they get from its impact on the other players, they will have a tendency to persevere in using such a style and enjoy it.

A more "emotional" style of engagement would be to fully give in to the vertigo created by completely engaging with the gravity of the virtual situation taking place in the exercise. For example, a retirement home threatened by rising waters or the report of an accident that happened to one of their emergency teams without knowing if anyone is hurt, or how badly, can create a feeling of fear in a player deeply immersed in the simulation, which we will discuss in the next section. However, in order to explore these emotions or just because they are curious, a player can by choice yield to these kinds of emotions and adopt a style of play that leaves them vulnerable to the goings-on of the scenario. The stakes for such a player might be to live the crisis exercise as a virtual experience, giving them a chance to feel strong emotions, better understand themself and master their emotions more effectively.

Finally, the "passive" or "fatalistic" mode of engagement will manifest by a certain passivity of the player in the way they play, waiting to react to events when they happen rather than trying to anticipate them or proactively devising protection against them. They will realize that chance has no place in the progression of the crisis scenario: in a crisis scenario properly managed by a training team, chance seems to intervene by the juxtaposition of crisis events at the worst times.

6.4. Managing Ludicity

6.4.1. *Observing and detecting Ludicity*

By its very nature, Ludicity, which is an underlying effect of the main activity of crisis management simulation, is hard to directly observe while being sure of not observing something else. Thus, the usual actions expected during a crisis rely on the coordination between players that follows a rational framework without requiring any Ludicity. They are nonetheless conducive to the engagement of the players beyond the minimum required to be operationally effective: how can we then distinguish between a zealous, but perfectly rational, use of operational rules dealing with the coordination between crisis managers and the unreasonable engagement of a player with their character to deal with the ludic stakes that they identified in the simulation?

Worse still, observing to check whether the participant in a crisis management exercise follows the proper use of best practices and operational rules in crisis management partially blinds the observer to the manifestation of Ludicity.

The first rule of observing the Ludicity of a crisis management exercise is to observe the room from the point of view of playing and to ignore what the players should do or should have done to properly react to the events inserted in the game space by the training team. The main aim is to observe the holistic experience created and lived by the players dealing with the crisis exercise from their point of view. At the end of the simulation, what the players will remember from this experience will not be in the form of a rational retelling of a series of trials and actions that succeeded or not, but rather in the form of a continuum mixing actions and emotions from the player with the events and incidents that influenced the decisions made individually and collectively. In other words, the scenario as perceived by the players can be quite different from what the training team thought they created and played.

To realize this, it is important for the training team to have either a direct link to the players through an ally among the players charged with reporting to the training team the experience of the simulation they are sharing with the players or an indirect link through observers present in the room who are able to observe and report their observations to the training team or through a CCTV system which requires constant scanning to detect the fleeting moment of play.

The second rule is to focus on the appearance of Ludicity and how its elements manifest themselves: ease of each player in playing their characters, diegetic spaces that are subdivided or whole, cognitive authority, and the degree and type of engagement of the players. This requires separating the observation of the Ludicity of the simulation from that of the rational parts of the management of the crisis, for example, by either alternating between distinct phases of the observation of Ludicity elements and of the rational actions of the exercise by one observer or entrusting each subject to different observers.

The third rule is to focus the observer's attention (in real time or after the facts) on the moments when the Ludicity is most in evidence, that is, most clearly itself with no possibility of confusing it with the normal manifestations of the rational management of the crisis. These elements are of two kinds: the start, suspension or end of the simulations and when a dissonance threatening the normal progress of the simulation happens.

6.4.2. *Using Ludicity to augment the simulation*

Awareness of the potential Ludicity of a crisis management exercise and knowing how to use it helps to modify the way simulations are created and enacted to augment the learning experience.

Thus, it is essential that each player is at ease as quickly as possible in playing their character so that the lost time at the start of the simulation, when the player is not yet fully able to play their character, is reduced as much as possible. This can be done by giving each player a character sheet, which gives not only the general aspects of the role to be played but also the details about crisis management competences that the player can use in the course of the simulation (Lappi 2004). Otherwise, it can be done by boosting the character sheet with competences proposed by the player, depending on their knowledge of crisis management, during a discussion with the game master before the start of the simulation. This would be quite close to the process of character creation in a role-playing game, enabling both the player to start projecting himself in the simulation to come and the game master to insert in the game appropriate ideas coming from the players. This kind of discussion also helps the game master to discern the mode or modes of engagement preferred by the players in order to eventually adapt to how they run the game.

In addition to this character creation, another way to reduce this lag at the start of the game when the players are getting into their character is to subject them very quickly to an initiation trial that will enable them to realize their own capabilities in the game. It must be an event that happens very early in the simulation and, more importantly, must be easy to sort for the players to avoid distracting them from the subsequent major events. The trap of these kinds of starting events is that players might think it to be a major event and start spending more time and energy on it that would be liked by the training team. The best solution might be to make them manage a false alert, which the game master can discard when needed.

Despite the fear it can create in a training team, because of the flamboyance it entails, the "theatrical" mode of engagement should be encouraged among the team of players but not necessarily from every player. In fact, this style of engagement pushes the other players to get more in the simulation and help them to express feelings which will enhance their learning experience (Jones 2004). To achieve this, we would first recommend adding to the character sheet an objective for the game so as to give the player a stake in the game based on past fictional experiences (in a role-playing game, we would call it "the background"). It can be something like: "As the person in charge of emergency services, you are still raw from the criticisms made by the population and the mayor during the previous crisis as to the lack of attention from the emergency services given to the concerns of the people affected by the crisis". It is then important to make each player see one another as their character as quickly and as fully as possible. If wearing some distinctive piece of clothing is not always possible, it is imperative that at least the names of each character are known by all with the rank attached, if needed. Most importantly, during the simulation, the training team must fully engage in theatrical interactions with the players who are comfortable with this type of engagement; this will encourage other players to follow suit.

The other types of engagement should not be forgotten. The training team must identify and use them, giving each player what they need: the egotistic player needs to feel that their achievements are recognized, the emotional player needs to feel fear with dilemmas and soul searching and the passive player's attention must be solicited more often than others.

By using the various types of engagement, the training team has a much better chance of creating a real group out of the players. They will ensure that the players have a shared view of the fictional situation (Badke-Schaub 2007) by pushing them to create a common representation that incorporates various viewpoints: creating or analyzing a map of the situation is one of the most efficient ways to do so (Röhl and Herbrick 2008); another possible tool is to write a summary of the situation. During such an exercise, or in case of a major incident during the simulation, the dissonance can threaten the simulation. If the training team has sufficiently increased the engagement of the players, they can hope that it will be enough to maintain the liminal space and get over the dissonance. However, it might become necessary to make use of the cognitive authority, which the training team has identified in the group, by giving the player the information or the game-out decisions, which will enable them to decree the end of the dissonance.

6.5. Conclusions

6.5.1. *Using Ludicity to mend the simulation*

By its design, a crisis management exercise can be analyzed from the point of view of a game. If the exercise is not an endless repetition of the same processes but is created to place the participants in an unfamiliar situation with no predefined solutions, one can see in it elements showing that the participants are playing without realizing it, and we will call this "Ludicity".

Beyond the elements that we have already discussed in this chapter (diegetic spaces, cognitive authorities, the type and degree of engagement of the players), the Ludicity of the game is also a force that binds the participants together in an animating part of the simulation that they inhabit. The strongest manifestation of this force is the fact that the simulation endures when a major dissonance occurs, either because of a mistake of the training team or a misunderstanding from some of the players threatens the collective representation of the fictional situation or simply because the training team suspends or terminates the simulation.

It is then noticeable that the players themselves keep the simulation alive in their imagination, while the training team repairs the break during the simulation or at the end of the simulation, for as long as the player needs to accept that the simulation is finished and they must step out of their character.

This should teach the training team that, after the initial lag, the simulation they are in charge of (and control) and the Ludicity of the game created by the players (which they control) get superimposed, and that the success of the exercise from the teaching point of view depends both on the proper flow of the simulation and on its congruence with the underlying Ludicity.

6.5.2. *Crisis exercise or crisis simulacrum: does the exercise imitate life or does life imitate the exercise?*

What finally distinguishes the exercise considered as a simulation and the exercise where its Ludicity is cultivated resides in what researchers looking into Nordic LARP (live action role-playing) tend to call "high definition simulations".

Through this notion proposed by Nordgren (2008), we can distinguish between low resolution simulations (which reproduce as faithfully as possible the way things happen, such as the re-enactment of a historical battle) and high resolution simulations (which enable the players to feel genuine emotions, such as the ones people in the real situation, which the simulation emulates, would feel). In other words, according to De Castel *et al.* (2014), we would distinguish between simulation (just like) and imitation (as if).

If the group of players is driven by one or more players playing in a theatrical or emotional mode, then participating in a crisis management simulation gives birth to emotions in the player which, according to our scale based on 30 primary emotions (Pelissolo *et al.* 2007), correlate at 90% to the ones experienced by people managing the real crisis. In this case, they are really what the Nordic LARP Players call a "high resolution simulation".

This correlation between a crisis management exercise and the management of a real crisis is disturbing: if we consider that the crisis managers that we are here talking about are not hardened professionals in crisis management (like firefighters or soldiers) but rather civil servants detached from their agencies to help in solving the crisis usually without any training other than experiences from their past crisis, we can wonder if it is not due to, contrary to our intuition, an adaptation of these people's behaviors while managing the crisis to how they believe they should behave in these situations, as they learned in simulations (Baudrillard 1981).

Finally, we can note that the 10% of diverging emotions between reality and simulation seem to be the pleasure taken by the participants in the simulation, which is not present in reality, and the fear, anxiety and goodwill felt in a real situation, which are not present in a simulation. It is important to note that this 10% difference between emotions felt in the simulation and in reality might not be an inveterate difference. It is simply that the fear felt and overcome in a simulation creates pleasure (Tammy *et al.* 2017), while the same fear when it is overcome in reality creates pride (Csíkszentmihályi 1990).

6.6. References

Badke-Schaub, P., Lauche, K., Neumann, A., and Ahmed, S. (2007). Task–team–process: Assessment and analysis of the development of shared representations in an engineering team. *Design Thinking Research Symposium 7: Design Meeting Protocols*, McDonnell, J. (ed.). Peter Lloyd, London, Central Saint Martins College of Art and Design and University of the Arts London, 97–111.

Baudrillard, J. (1981). *Simulacres et simulations*. Galilée, Paris.

Boin, A., Kofman-Bos, C., and Overdijk, W., (2004). Crisis simulations: Exploring tomorrow's vulnerabilities and threats. *Simul. Gaming*, 35(3), 378–393.

Caillois, R. (1958). *Les jeux et les hommes. Le masque et le vertige*. Gallimard, Paris.

Carenzo, L., Ragozzino, F., Colombo, D., Barra, F.L., Della, C.F., and Ingrassia, P.I. (2016) Virtual laboratory and imaging: An online simulation tool to enhance hospital disaster preparedness training experience. *Eur. J. Emerg. Med.*

Chowanda, A., Flintham, M., Blanchfield, P., and Valstar, M., (2016). Playing with Social and Emotional Game Companions, *16th International Conference on Intelligent Virtual Agents, IVA*, September 20–23, Los Angeles, CA, USA, pp. 85–95.

Csikszentmihalyi, M. (1990). *Flow: The Psychology of Optimal Experience*. Haper & Row, New York, NY.

Daniau, S., (2005). Jeu de rôles formatif et maturation des adultes. PhD Thesis, Paul Valery University, Montpellier III.

De Castel, S., Jenson, J., and Thumlert, K., (2014). From simulation to imitation: Controllers, corporeality, and mimetic play. *Simul. Gaming*, 45(3), 332–355.

Franck, A. (2012), Gaming the game: A study of the gamer mode in educational wargaming. *Simul. Gaming*, 43(I), 118–132.

Goutx, D. (2014). Réaliser la gravité d'enjeux abstraits à travers une simulation : comprendre COP-RW comme un rite de passage. *Négociations*, 2014/2(22), 17–28. doi:10.3917/neg.022.0017, available: https://www.cairn.info/revue-negociations-2014-2-page-17.htm.

Gredler, M.E. (2004). Games and simulations and their relationships to learning, Games/simulations and learning, In *Handbook of Research on Educational Communications and Technology*, Jonassen, D.H. (ed.). Lawrence Erlbaum Associates Publishers, Mahwah.

Harviainen, T., (2012). Ritualistic games, boundary control, and information uncertainty. *Simul. Gaming.* 43(4), 506–527.

Harviainen, T. and Lieberoth, A. (2012). Similarity of social information processes in games and rituals: Interfaces. *Simul. Gaming*, 43(4), 528–549.

Henriot, J. (1989). *Sous couleur de jouer, la métaphore ludique.* Editions José Corti, Paris.

Hitchens, M. and Drachen, A. (2009). The many faces of role-playing games. *Int. J. Role-Playing*, 1(1), 3–21.

Hopeametsä, H. (2008). 24 hours in a bomb shelter: player, character and immersion in ground zero. In *Playground Worlds: Creating and Evaluating Experiences of Role-playing Games*, Montola, M. and Stenros, J. (eds). Solmukohta.

Huizinga, J. (1938). *Homo ludens, essai sur la fonction sociale du jeu.* Gallimard, Paris.

Jones, K., (2004). Fear of emotions. *Simul. Gaming*, 35(4), 454–460.

Kapp, S. (2013). L'immersion fictionnelle collaborative. Une étude de la posture d'engagement dans les jeux de rôles grandeur nature. PhD Thesis, Université Libre de Bruxelles.

Lantis J.S. (1998). Simulations and experiential learning in the international relations classroom. *Int. Negot.*, 1998/3, 39–57.

Lappi, A.-P. (2004). The character interpretation the process before the immersion and the game. In *Beyond Role and Play Tools, Toys and Theory for Harnessing the Imagination*, Montola, M. and Stenros, J. (eds). Ropecon, Helsinki.

Lieberoth, A., (2014). Shallow gamification: Testing psychological effects of framing an activity as a game. *Games Cult.*, 10(3), https://doi.org/10.1177/1555412014559978, 1–20.

McGonigal, J. (2003). A real little game: The Pinocchio effect in pervasive play. Lecture notes, available: http://www.avantgame.com.

Morissette, J.-F. (2010). Le jeu dans la sociologie. Du phénomène au concept. PhD Thesis, University of Quebec.

Nakamura, J., Csikszentmihalyi, M. (2002). The concept of flow. In *Handbook of Positive Psychology*, Snyder, C.R. and Lopez, S.J. (eds.), University Press, Oxford.

Nordgren, A. (2008). High resolution larping: Enabling subtlety at totem and beyond. In *Playground Worlds: Creating and Evaluating Experiences of Role-playing Games*, Montola, M. and Stenros, J. (eds). Solmukohta.

Pélissolo, A., Rolland, J.-P., Perez-Diaz, F., Allilaire, J.-F. (2007). Evaluation dimensionnelle des émotions en psychiatrie : validation du questionnaire Emotionnalité positive et négative à 31 items (EPN-31). *L'Encéphale*, 1(33), 256–263.

Röhl, T. and Herbrik, R. (2008). Mapping the imaginary–maps in fantasy role-playing games. *Forum Qual. Sozialforschung/Forum: Qual. Soc. Res.*, 9(3), available: http://nbn-resolving.de/urn:nbn:dc:0114-fqs0803255.

Shernoff, D.J., Hamari, J., and Rowe, E. (2014). Measuring flow in educational games and gamified learning environments. *EdMedia*, June 23–26, Tampere, Finland.

Smith, D. (2004). For whom the bell tolls: Imagining accidents and the development of crisis simulation in organizations. *Simul. Gaming*, 35(3), 347–362.

Stavroulia, K.E., Makri-Botsari, E., Psycharis, S., Kekkeris, G. (2016) Emotional experiences in simulated classroom training environments, *Int. J. Inf. Learn. Technol.*, 33(3), 172–185.

Suits, B. (2014). *The Grasshopper. Games, Life and Utopia*, 3rd edition. Broadview Press, Parution.

Sussking, L.E. and Corburn, J. (1999). Using simulations to teach negotiation : Pedagogical theory and practise, Working Paper, Harvard Law School.

Szilas, N. and Sutter, W.D. (2009). Mieux comprendre la notion d'intégration entre l'apprentissage et le jeu. Actes d'Environnements Informatiques pour l'Apprentissage Humain EIAH09, Serious Games Workshop. Le Mans, 23 June, France, pp. 27–40.

Tammy, L.J.-H., Wu, D.-Y., and Tao, C.-C. (2017). So scary, yet so fun: The role of self-efficacy in enjoyment of a virtual reality horror game. *New Media Soc.*, available: https://doi.org/10.1177/14614448177 44850.

Tychsen, A., McIlwain, D., Brolund, T., Hitchens, M., (2007). Player-character dynamics in multi-player role playing games, In *3rd Digital Games Research Association International Conference: "Situated Play"*, Akira, B. (ed.). DiGRA, Finland, 40–48.

Van Gennep, A. (1909). *Les rites de passage*. Dunod, Paris.

Van Schaik, P., Martin, S., Vallance, M. (2012). Measuring flow experience in an immersive virtual environment for collaborative learning. *J. Comput. Assist. Learn.*, 28, 350–365.

Waskul, D. and Lust, M. (2004). Role-playing and playing roles: The person, player, and persona in fantasy role-playing, symbolic interaction. *Soc. Study Symbol. Interact.*, 27(3), 333–356.

7

Digital Training for Authorities: What is the Best Way to Communicate During a Crisis?

A crisis can be defined as "the perception of an unpredictable event that threatens important expectancies of stakeholders and can seriously impact an organization's performance and generate negative outcomes" (Coombs 2007). When a disaster occurs, an organization that moves from a normal to a crisis state must first meet their social responsibility challenges (Coombs and Holladay 2015) and focus on responding to the crisis (Haddow and Haddow 2014). Several authors have highlighted the importance of preparedness in allowing good crisis management. For instance, Avery *et al.* (2016) interviewed 307 public crisis managers who managed one or more crises. Given the severity of the crises managed by these actors, the more they claimed being prepared for it, the more satisfied they were with the management performed. Not all organizations are equal with regard to their crisis management preparedness: there are differences in their size (Johansen *et al.* 2012) and between rural and urban settings. Particularly, when a major crisis has already occurred, public managers are more likely to be better prepared for the next one (Avery *et al.* 2016).

Chapter written by Clément LAVERDET, Karine WEISS, Aurélia BONY-DANDRIEUX, Jérôme TIXIER and Serge CAPAROS.

During a crisis, the importance of communication in the management of the crisis has been emphasized by several authors (e.g. Coombs and Holladay 2010). To meet their crisis management objectives, organizations must communicate to populations in a timely manner (Haddow and Haddow 2014). After a crisis has ended, crisis managers should then fall within a learning phase, in which members of the organization should provide critical feedback on their crisis management of the event (Mitroff 1994). This learning phase enhances the organization's ability to manage future crises.

In this chapter, we want to standardize some of the analyses performed on crisis management to produce a comprehensive report on the quality of the crisis communication delivered. This report may be produced following a real situation or during an emergency response drill. Usually, users' reactions are not realistically reproduced during a drill. We suggest a state of the art focused on the measurement of the crisis communication quality released, and then we set up an example of monitoring, without taking into account audience reactions. This report can be delivered to the manager during or after a safety drill or real-life emergency. This report may be considered as monitoring if available in real time. If conducted after the crisis, this report is considered a detail of a critical event analysis, called "feedback on the experience (REX)" in French civil security.

7.1. What is a good crisis communication?

The emergency of a crisis generally results in the need for up-to-date and accurate information. Information about the event is valued, and managers are asked by journalists to quickly deliver information to the public (van der Meer *et al.* 2017). To our knowledge, no authority directly monitors the quality of crisis communications delivered by crisis stakeholders.

Several authors have suggested "good practices" to implement in crisis communication (e.g. Khan 2017; Haddow and Haddow 2014; Seeger 2006). Such practices are part of the operational use implemented by some nations (e.g. Australian Office of Emergency Management and Australian State Emergency Management

Committee 2017 or Lerchs *et al.* 2017 in Belgium). Several public managers have contributed to this approach of good practices (e.g. Schwarzenegger 2004), such as some private organizations (e.g. International Air Transport Association 2014). As generic elements, these good practices apply to all crisis situations, according to the manager's best judgment.

In general, a regular and responsive communication is essential (Haddow and Haddow 2014). On the one hand, regular updates and reviews should be published, particularly to reduce media pressure. On the other hand, in order to meet the specific challenges of crisis management, the authority must communicate the relevant elements from the populations' viewpoint – mainly information that enables to have a comprehensive representation of the situation and/or the threat as well as behaviors to reduce the threat (e.g. Parmer *et al.* 2016; Valls *et al.* 2014b). Ideally, these two types of communications are set up as a high priority at the earliest: other communications that do not directly meet the organization's ethical objectives (e.g. repair the organization's image) should not be issued until the societal objectives of crisis management are met by the manager (Coombs and Holladay 2015). During the crisis, the manager must be able to provide a full source of information in their own right by proactively issuing crisis communications and activating broadcasting partnerships, particularly in cooperation with local media and influencers (Haddow and Haddow 2014; Palttala and Vos 2012).

Alerting the public is one of the authorities' main responsibility when a crisis threatens civil security (Valls *et al.* 2014b), and several authors have formulated recommendations for dealing with this alerting phase, which should be repeated regularly (Lagadec 1991). More specifically, some authors have suggested specific actions that the communicant should undertake in order to give early warning. For Palttala and Vos (2012), "alerts […] are provided in a timely manner and their content is well checked; stand out to attract attention; give clear instructions for action to reduce the likelihood of harm; include advice on how to find more information; encourage people to contact persons who might not know of the warning". In addition, the authors have suggested informing the media of warning messages and monitoring the audience's reactions to instructions and warning messages.

During a crisis, people tend to inform themselves or communicate through channels that they were already familiar with before the crisis (Steelman *et al.* 2015), provided that it is available during the crisis. During certain crises, word-of-mouth is the main source of information for populations (e.g. Austin *et al.* 2012). It is therefore necessary to communicate according to the habits and information sources of the audience. This involves preparation for communication in normal circumstances. For instance, Palttala and Vos (2012) propose an operational framework to prepare authorities for crisis communication, including "knowing the public groups and their media use habits. The various public groups are identified according to how they seek and receive information about risks". Other authors have suggested the identification of opinion leaders (Haddow and Haddow 2014) as relays for crisis communications. Besides, public organizations (e.g. universities) can directly communicate or relay crisis communications of the authority (Omilion-Hodges and McClain 2016), just like any other traditional means of communication which makes it possible to reach an audience (Valls *et al.* 2014a). Thus, electronic word-of-mouth reinforces traditional word-of-mouth communication in the dissemination of crisis communications to populations: they redirect crisis information.

The usefulness of social networks in emergency management has been highlighted by previous studies. Such networks support different communication functions that benefit all crisis stakeholders, in all phases of the crisis management process (Houston *et al.* 2014). Ultimately, social networks support communication and information gathering in a way that complements traditional channels, whether for emergency managers, media or populations. Moreover, crisis managers seem to suspect the relevance of these tools, and those who claim to control social networks tend to believe that they are capable of responding effectively to a crisis (Graham *et al.* 2015).

Some digital channels have features that are particularly relevant to crisis communicators, such as the number of connected users, the fluidity of information dissemination, the interactive nature and richness of the content that can be published and the ability to plan multiple broadcasting at different times. Far from being trivial, the features of digital tools make them invaluable in most emergency situations. Such features include the long-term availability of contents after they have been released or the possibility to collect some data, including reactions to published contents.

At present, among all the digital tools available, Facebook seems to be essential for supporting effective crisis communication because of its large audience and the public's habits of reading and sharing information (Newman *et al.* 2016). In fact, some organizations have recommended communicating on Facebook as a priority during crisis management: for the International Air Transport Association (2014), any message sent outside this platform must also lead to one or more Facebook post(s). Ultimately, communication to the public is only one of the means to effectively meet the objectives of crisis management.

7.2. Information dissemination

The manager expects the people to perform several behaviors during a crisis, such as sharing crisis messages by word-of-mouth. While press releases are often taken up (paraphrased or quoted) by the media, shared Facebook posts or retweets result in carbon copies, including acknowledgment of the source and a potential message from the sharing entity. On Facebook, the contents are shared as it triggers physiological arousal (Berger 2011), when the sharing is consistent with the self of the user (Kim and Yang 2017), that is, the image of him/her to which he/she adheres and which he/she puts forward. It is assumed that the share of crisis messages in which the content may be relevant to others is shared altruistically, implying that crisis-related content sharing is consistent with the self of most users if the content has a high informative value.

If we disregard the message content, the number of entry points into the network will determine the distribution of a message (Wang *et al.* 2012). To ensure a solid ground for digital word-of-mouth, authorities should focus on increasing their number of entry points for their communications. In other words, the objective of emergency communications should be broadcast locally by as many entities as possible, on as many channels as possible: from Facebook users to media organizations.

7.3. Behavioral communication

In order to take advantage of the potential of social networks, particularly in terms of dissemination, it is necessary to focus on the communications needed to respond to the crisis: delivering useful, rich and detailed information for the protection of populations. Some authors have suggested other good practices to implement with social networks, such as publishing links to a richer content (Freberg *et al.* 2013), involving the audience in the response to the crisis (Keim and Noji 2011) or even engaging in dialogue with them (Rowe and Frewer 2005). For this purpose, the manager can post questions on social networks in order to obtain information by monitoring comments or answers from the audience. By using social media in general, especially Facebook, an organization can also keep track of the answers to questions raised by other actors, or even suggest questions to publish in order to study the users' answers, especially if the other actors' audience is larger than that of the organization itself. For the analyst, it is a way to collect specific information.

Sometimes, managers implicitly expect populations to undertake specific actions such as disseminating crisis communications. However, there are two prerequisites for all behaviors to be initiated: they must make sense and be feasible (Heimlich 2010). Some behaviors do not make sense for all. For instance, when the authority asks people not to make phone calls so as not to overcrowd networks, the link between "hearing from family members" and "stopping someone from reaching emergency services" does not make sense for everyone. Other situations involve less significance associated with behaviors delivered by the authority, such as the danger announced as such but ignored because it seems familiar to the audience (e.g. "treacherous risk", Dedieu 2009) or when the authority minimizes the risk incorrectly (e.g. "situation under control" before the impact of a crisis event).

Previous research gave several behavioral communication techniques, including thinking about the most appropriate method according to the costs and benefits associated with behavior (Schultz 2014), as well as communicating precisely by accurately resuming the desired behavior and, if possible, leaving the message close to where the behavior is performed (Geller *et al.* 1982). Behaviors that do not make sense require an awareness campaign in normal circumstances, and the importance of prevention has been pointed out in several research studies, particularly to highlight the goals associated with each behavior (e.g. Schultz 2010). Scholars have suggested other concepts (e.g. Geller 1995). Communicators are asked to define their communication objectives and to put themselves in the position of the audience when defining the most appropriate message, regardless of the rules used to determine the most appropriate communication.

In this study, we propose an analysis that defines crisis communication from a public organization. This analysis is applicable when an organization communicates, whether in an emergency response drill or in a real emergency situation. Among the main French crises of 2017, we identified and qualified one of the situations which seemed to have had the greatest impact on a given local French prefecture (county authority). A prefecture is a public organization that typically manages a major disaster in its territory, along with other French civil security actors (cities, public services, etc.). We describe what we consider notable elements within the organization's editorial line and underline some possible improvements.

7.4. Method

This work is focused on Facebook communications. On February 1, 2018, we used the R software to collect the 2017 Facebook posts from 87 French prefectures and French sub-county prefectures that use Facebook. Given that the posts were collected after the crisis had happened, we could only collect data from posts that had not been deleted at the time of data collection: a total of 40,127 posts were collected. The major crisis that these organizations respond to leads to peaks in some of their Facebook data, including their publication frequency and the sharing of their posts by users or pages. Among the crises that trigger these sudden and particularly significant variations in the number of posts are the hurricanes known as IRMA, JOSE or MARIA, which affected several French prefectures. In comparison with their normal publications and the reactions of the audience to these publications, we chose the prefecture which seemed to have the most affected editorial line because of a crisis: *the prefecture of St. Barthélemy and St. Martin*. These islands were particularly affected by the tropical hurricanes of 2017, and the sharing of the prefecture's posts was more important at this specific time than in normal times.

First, we will summarize the situation and define the prefecture's crisis communication. Then, we will detail several indicators specific to the content communicated by the prefecture, more specifically the informative richness of its editorial line, the presence of explicit disseminating guidelines and the highlighting of the fact that mentioning the organization is not necessary for crisis communication. Moreover, the number of precise behaviors provided for each message is counted. This study focuses on providing feedback to managers after an emergency response drill: users' reactions to this real situation are not detailed.

7.5. Results

7.5.1. *Situation report*

St. Martin has a population of 78,000 including 35,000 on the French side. St. Barthélemy has 10,000 inhabitants. Hurricane IRMA developed from August 30 to September 12, 2017 and destroyed most of *St. Martin's* infrastructures and *St. Barthélemy* to a lesser extent. Regarding the island of St. Martin, the French Prime Minister reported

"95% of the houses [are] affected [...] and 60% uninhabitable" after IRMA. Most parts of the islands suffered a network interruption after IRMA (electricity, water, waste, etc.). Later on, Hurricane JOSE followed. Authorities were worried and also communicated about this subject. Ultimately, JOSE passed around 130 km from the islands, leading to lower winds than expected on the aforementioned islands. Afterwards, Hurricane MARIA was notified by the authorities as a major hazard, although it passed 150 km off the coasts of these islands. An urgent drinking-water crisis situation was still communicated after MARIA: the water carried by the network was still non-potable. Meanwhile, recovery or reconstruction was progressing on the islands. Then, until the end of 2017, the authorities communicated the disaster recovery plan, the resumption of activities and even critical event analysis. The recovery has not yet been achieved by this date (March 2018), especially on St. Martin, regarding the state of the water network and the built environment.

7.5.2. Editorial line: normal and crisis times

The communications issued from St. Martin and St. Barthélemy's prefecture in 2017 could be classified into different periods. On Facebook, the 297 posts published by the prefecture in 2017 are classified according to nine periods. The first part of the posts is considered as pre-IRMA: no information on tropical storms IRMA, HARVEY and MARIA were communicated, although the prefecture communicated and managed several meteorological events during this period, in May 2017 for instance. The pre-IRMA period (#1) stretches from January 1 to August 16.

Between August 16 and September 3, the prefecture published 10 posts, three of which were related to tropical storms or the upcoming cyclone season. The interval between these three posts about tropical storms or the hurricane season falls into an early warning period (#2), even though the intensity and the nature of the upcoming crisis was not directly appreciable in these posts. During this period of early warning, the islands were placed under "Yellow vigilance" (level 2 out of 4 of the French meteorological vigilance level, 4 being the highest) with the risk of "heavy rain and storms" by the prefecture on August 27, a few days before the first communications on IRMA.

The period from September 3 to September 6 corresponds to the period during which IRMA (#3) was reported as a threat to the islands, from the first cyclonic vigilance until the hurricane hit the islands. Most of the communications that followed were related to the crises studied (IRMA, JOSE and MARIA) and included protective behaviors intended for the populations, and even links to additional content.

The hurricane passed through the islands on September 6, causing a power outage (#4) and stopping the editorial line on Facebook until September 8. During this period, the prefecture did not communicate, although other organizations ensured the continuity of the prefectural crisis editorial line. For instance, Guadeloupe's prefecture published a situation report on the islands in question on September 6 at around 7:30 am, announcing that St. Barthélemy and St. Martin's prefectures were partly destroyed, hence the confinement of the prefect and her team. In the same vein, other media quoted or mentioned the prefecture, and, in the absence of electricity, it could still communicate in the field, among other channels available on the ground.

From September 8 onwards, the prefectural editorial line resumed, and the approach of hurricane JOSE (#5) was announced. The prefecture warned, in particular, about the risk of flying debris left by IRMA and resumed some of the instructions concerning tropical storms, which had already been distributed when IRMA occurred.

We define the entry into a recovery phase (#6) with the prefectural communication that gave information about the distance of JOSE on September 10. Early communications in this recovery phase included behaviors in order to reduce threats left by IRMA and JOSE, and, among other things, included security instructions on IRMA's risks of flying debris by tropical winds, despite the apparent distance of JOSE. Various posts related to the recovery followed IRMA and JOSE.

The approach of MARIA, then classified as a tropical storm, was communicated for the first time by the prefecture on September 17. Between September 17 and 20, the prefecture communicated about MARIA (#7), warning about the hurricane passing offshore of the islands.

Between September 20 and 25, following MARIA's passage, the prefecture adopted an editorial line that corresponds to a "resolution phase" of the crisis (#8), which should be defined according to the dates of the first and last communications, explicitly mentioning the non-potable nature of the water conveyed by the networks. Thus, September 20 corresponds to the continuation of the drinking-water crisis situation which was highlighted in the prefectural editorial line by communicating about the non-potable nature of water and the associated behaviors and information, to comprehend or reduce this threat, among other behaviors and information related to meteorological crises communicated so far.

On September 20, the prefecture sent six posts on the alert or vigilance level set by the prefecture with regard to the distance of MARIA, the non-potable and dangerous nature of water from the networks (associated with behaviors to reduce or avoid this threat) and circulation restrictions. From September 21, communications were related to the resumption of services and economic activities, the feedback on the incident and other information from the recovery phase. The prefecture explicitly communicated the non-potable nature of the water until September 25.

September 25 corresponds to the creation of an editorial line exclusively related to the reconstruction phase (#9), that is, which does not include behaviors or explicit instructions to reduce the threat of storms. The reconstruction phase is defined according to the changing style of the prefecture communications on the non-potable water, communicated from September 25 on the feedback on the event or the storytelling of the crisis management. Communications in the reconstruction phase were less urgent than before: they were purely informative. Other meteorological events could be communicated during this reconstruction phase, as in the pre-IRMA period (#1).

7.5.3. *Quality of communication*

Table 7.1 presents these periods and some characteristics of the prefecture's editorial line: the first and last post published over the period, the duration in days, the number of posts issued, the frequency of publication, etc. The fourth period corresponds to a power outage on the islands and did not generate any prefectural post on Facebook, which is not presented in the table.

Period	First post	Last post	Duration (#day)	Number of posts	Posts by day	Mean words by post	Content with text and link
1 Pre-IRMA	2017-01-04 14:44:35	2017-08-08 16:28:01	216.1	144	0.67	62.2	83
2 Early Warning	2017-08-16 21:47:37	2017-08-31 21:11:48	15.0	10	0.67	48.9	8
3 IRMA	2017-09-03 10:50:25	2017-09-06 06:46:22	2.8	18	6.43	148.6	5
5 JOSE	2017-09-08 14:48:26	2017-09-10 01:29:55	1.4	11	7.86	103.1	3
6 Recuperation	2017-09-11 15:03:36	2017-09-16 20:06:41	5.2	30	5.77	60.9	20
7 MARIA	2017-09-17 11:44:50	2017-09-20 12:47:38	3.0	10	3.33	158.2	9
8 Resolution	2017-09-20 13:16:42	2017-09-24 18:14:35	4.2	16	3.81	66.9	13
9 Reconstruction	2017-09-25 00:05:38	2017-12-26 17:23:15	92.7	58	0.63	72.0	27

Table 7.1. *Content posted by the prefecture*

The elements presented in Table 7.1 are defined according to prefectural communications and are available in emergency situations as well as in an emergency response drill. In a real emergency situation, the elements presented could be enriched by users' reactions, bringing new forms of assessment of the crisis communication quality (interacting with the populations, introducing questions or monitoring the answers to public questions or reactions to content, etc.). In addition, the manager's private data (for example, through Facebook Insights) is a significant contribution to this type of feedback on crisis communication. All of these data must be presented in order to give a more detailed report on the situation, especially on the diffusion of prefectural communications during these different periods.

In this emergency situation, we can see that the prefecture communicated more frequently during the most urgent phases of the crisis. Apart from the power outage period, all the other periods where posts mentioned IRMA, JOSE and MARIA hazards generated several posts per day, and only pre-crisis, early warning and reconstruction periods generated less than one post per day, on average. This effect of major crises on the organization's editorial line that manages them is typical. This organization is considered as one of the prefectures' communications most affected by a crisis in 2017, particularly in terms of publication frequency. This high frequency is in accordance with the good practices of crisis communication (e.g. Haddow and Haddow 2014) and reflects a crisis management operation concerned about informing people through the organization's Facebook page.

Regarding the published messages, they are longer and more detailed when the prefecture directly communicates about the risks related to the crises: this is a consequence of the detailed information on the situation and the numerous behaviors specific to the situation communicated by the prefecture in most of its posts related to the crisis. Other indicators of the richness of communications support this result, as the prefecture tends to include links to additional content when communicating in emergency situations, especially for JOSE and MARIA.

Figure 7.1 shows the distribution of the number of posts from the prefecture. The colors of the bars represent the different types of content published, for each week (top) or each day of the crisis situation (bottom). The day of the passage of the hurricane is represented by a vertical dotted line. The phases of the crisis defined according to prefectural communications are indicated by a horizontal line, for example the red line begins with the first Facebook post mentioning IRMA and extends to the last post issued on the subject.

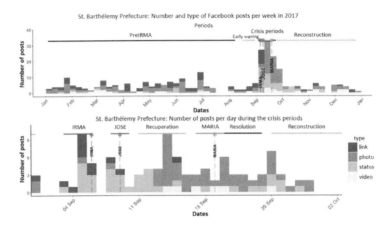

Figure 7.1. *Defined periods and Facebook posts of the prefecture of St. Barthélemy and St. Martin: type and frequency of publication in 2017 per week (top), and during emergency situations per day (bottom). For a color version of this figure, see www.iste.co.uk/sauvagnargues/crisis.zip*

The prefecture communicated the dangers associated with JOSE and MARIA until after the hurricane hit the islands: the impact of these crises led to communications, especially about the risks still incurred and about the situation or its evolution. Then, these crises led to resolution and reconstruction communications. However, the time period during which the IRMA warning was issued is limited: the first communication explicitly mentioning the cyclonic risk to come was posted 3 days before its passage by the prefecture and the publication rate was only particularly high from September 5. Here, the prefecture's Facebook page is slow to enter into a crisis Facebook editorial line, which came up 3 days before the hurricane hit the islands. Next, the crisis editorial line was regularly updated, from the first communications about JOSE: the effect of a previous crisis had an impact on the frequency of prefectural publications for the following ones.

7.5.4. *Defining a crisis editorial line*

Most messages sent by this authority during a crisis contain relevant facts for the user: detailed information or behaviors to deal with the situation. As always, in terms of communication, improvements can be made, especially by identifying missing or unnecessary facts or by suggesting alternative formulations.

We first present the message that marks the entry point to the period where the prefectural editorial line is related to IRMA (#3) (see the following) before focusing on its positive and negative aspects. The message is a cyclonic vigilance issued on September 3, following the "Heavy rain and storms" vigilance published a few days prior:

> Saint Barthélemy and Saint Martin are placed on "hurricane" yellow alert. JMI1: stay alert and stay informed on the cyclone's evolution by listening to the weather reports; JMI2: check the necessary reserves (food, water, candles, batteries, medicines...); JMI3: check your radio station and its power supply (batteries); JMI4: avoid long outings; JMI5: do not set sail for a long time if no special obligation http://www.meteofrance.gp /vigilance-antilles-guyane[1].

The relevant facts of the message from a user's perspective are the first sentence of the message is a catchphrase which recalls: the places involved and the situation; the behaviors mentioned, which represent 78% of the message; the website link to another source (MétéoFrance) providing more detailed information, and no irrelevant topic in an emergency situation[2] is noticeable. These elements (attention getter, behaviors, link to external content and only relevant content) are relevant in a crisis editorial line.

Thereafter and for this type of list, each of the specific behavioral facts found in a message is classified as behavior. Here, the message

---

1 This message is a Facebook post from the *Préfecture de Saint-Barthélemy et de Saint-Martin*'s official page, available at: https://www.facebook.com/prefet971/ posts/1410407245740056.
2 For example, organizational propaganda or other promotion of the official authority with no informative value on the event.

contains eight specific behaviors that apply to all (check the weather forecast, anticipate food and water reserves, etc.) and the order on sailing. A distinction is made between some facts, since they seem to apply to a specific audience (e.g. not to set sail) or to be unclear (e.g. to stay vigilant), but we consider the ban to apply to everyone as a specific behavior.

Several suggestions on improvements can be made in terms of the wording used. For instance, this message does not include an explicit dissemination order, contains information not related to the crisis (JMI1, JMI2, etc.) and is not a behavioral order but a list of behaviors, among other details which limit the quality of the message.

It is important to be aware that in a real emergency, such feedback is enhanced by dissemination. For instance, this post was shared 14 times by users and twice by pages. While the overall quality of the message is satisfactory, the message dissemination is particularly weak. In this regard, users' feedback is essential to ensure the quality of crisis communication dissemination, among other possibilities.

7.5.5. Behavior, dissemination orders and crisis storytelling

Figure 7.2 shows the posts published by the prefecture according to the number of behaviors they propose to the populations. The colors indicate the levels of vigilance communicated by the prefecture, and the remaining communications are in black.

The prefecture communicated several weather warnings. In the pre-IRMA or early-warning period, 12 yellow and 1 red alerts were issued. In September, the prefecture released 20 warnings, among other crisis communications. These alert levels are of different colors, depending on the gravity of the situation: the authority reported a high alert level (orange to violet) during the passage of the storms, and then notified an end of alert (grey) after MARIA. It also published behavior lists with almost all of its weather warnings, even in normal circumstances (yellow). This is an excellent practice that the prefecture often applies. During acute crisis periods, the prefecture communicated behaviors in 40 of the 85 posts it sent out. These

40 posts included almost five behaviors, on average. Since the prefecture also tended to publish situation updates and detailed information, its editorial line was remarkably rich and relevant for the users, with regard to its quality.

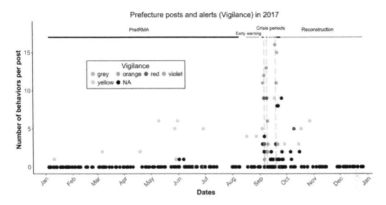

Figure 7.2. *Facebook posts of St. Barthélemy and St. Martin in 2017: number of specific behaviors in the message and official alerts posted on Facebook. For a color version of this figure, see www.iste.co.uk/sauvagnargues/crisis.zip*

In order to support the dissemination of its communications, the prefecture tended to rarely use an explicit dissemination order such as "share this information". In 2017, only nine posts of the prefecture contained an explicit dissemination order. These posts were related to one of the crises studied and were issued between September 5 and 17. Usually, the dissemination order was put at the end of the message. One improvement strategy would be to frequently use a dissemination order as an attention getter for the most important communications.

Other qualitative indicators can be appreciated, such as the presence of useless facts for the user in a crisis editorial line. The prefecture highlighted the representatives of public authorities or a private organization in seven posts issued before September 25: few crisis communications put forward an organization before a reconstruction editorial line, which was positive. The first presentations of organizations were issued during the reconstruction following IRMA. Then, the storytelling of crisis managers was rather communicated in the reconstruction phase following MARIA. This was quite late, as some organizational crisis managers tended to communicate in order to maintain their image at an early stage, sometimes breaking the good practices of crisis communication.

In terms of crisis communication, the usefulness of these points for users is sometimes arguable. The content published by this prefecture varied from an iconic communication of the political storytelling in which a member of the French executive or politicians can engage, from a simple quote of the clearance services to a crisis management. This focus on "State services" in a vigilance and warning message (orange and red) could have been reformulated in a less injurious manner: it could have been more concise and informative. It was therefore inappropriate to mention it in an informative communication on the situation. Informing about the situation by mentioning an organization increases the risk of introducing irrelevant content for the user in a communication, which ruins an editorial line of crisis response and generally slows down dissemination: sharing content that includes an organization name is generally less in agreement with the user's self, used to suppress their reactions as soon as they guess the slightest advertising content (e.g. on Facebook: Boerman *et al.* 2017). The more useful a message is to users, the more organization highlighting can be considered harmful. In this state of mind, the appropriate way of mentioning an organization during an emergency requires that this mention is directly useful to the users (e.g. indicating a food distribution at the organization's address or a non-profit emergency service set up by this organization). Since users control the content they share, it is particularly injurious to mention an organization in a crisis communication that is useful to populations, delivering detailed information or protective behaviors. On the contrary, it is difficult to quantify the negative nature of a post of pure storytelling about crisis management issued once the issues related to corporate social responsibility are addressed. Similarly, when a communication does not involve any sharing or reaction from the users, the impact on populations is limited because of the reduced audience.

7.6. Summary

The content communicated on Facebook by the prefecture was particularly informative on the situation. Although the prefecture was slow to enter into a crisis editorial line on Facebook, it implemented some good practices in crisis communication. It especially issued many warnings during normal periods as well as long lists of behaviors to reduce the threat in most crisis communications, which was particularly noticeable. In addition, the prefecture frequently communicated from IRMA's approach, after which it maintained a rich and detailed crisis editorial line. The emphasis on organization is limited to reconstruction, which is a wise use of crisis storytelling. As always in terms of communication, improvements can be made. The main objective here is to support the dissemination of prefectural communications on Facebook by activating dissemination partnerships and publishing contents adapted to be widely disseminated, especially by explicitly asking users to share messages. Other recommendations may be made on the wording used, such as the unnecessary content in some crisis posts or the non-injunctive nature of the behaviors communicated.

7.7. Limits

As with most works on the critical analysis of crisis situations, this work needs to be highlighted with more detailed data from stakeholders (feedback on the crisis or the emergency response drill) and is complementary to an analysis including other channels: in particular, outside the scope of the study where stakeholders can communicate in the field or by being quoted in the media, for instance. On the other hand, it is necessary to define with the manager the relevance of the various criteria established, according to the situation and its objectives.

Data on users' reactions or organizations are not usually presented in an emergency response drill. In this way, the focus is on feedback that can be given to an organization that communicates without any interest on users' reactions. Consequently, the criteria used to categorize issued crisis communications (e.g. Parmer *et al.* 2016) or the managers' actions (e.g. Palttala and Vos, 2012) deserve to be compared with the actual dissemination of communications (e.g. Arif *et al.* 2016), to further qualify these communications or editorial lines, and especially their general tendency to be shared by users.

7.8. Conclusion

There is no perfect editorial line, especially in crisis communication where efficiency criteria are open to debate. The digital is a source of information in emergency situations, at least to study the crisis editorial lines and associated users' reactions. This type of feedback allows managers to practice their critical thinking skills with regard to the quality of their crisis communications. Here, this prefecture provided crisis information of excellent quality regarding its usefulness for users, although the content communicated in an emergency situation can always be improved, such as the speed at which communications are disseminated. To the credit of a rapid and systematic return on the digital communication of organizations, it is indicated that contents published promptly after or before the impact of a crisis are susceptible to being erased by the authority (out-of-date reports, etc.). If communications are not stored, the erasing of crisis communication is incompatible with a learning phase and truncates this type of return.

By generalizing this type of analysis to several crisis managers and channels, emergency communications are documented. This seems essential in the sense that the crisis communication section is, to our knowledge, often underdeveloped or even non-existent in the critical analysis of a crisis or an emergency response drill. Overall, our thesis work emphasizes the quality of French prefectural communications during a major crisis on the French territory (between 2016 and 2018), although the dissemination of their communications was sometimes reduced. On the one hand, the prefectures were generally highlighted and more shared by the audience after a major crisis, compared to the media who cover the event. On the other hand, prefectural disseminations are less significant than those of the press (by their Facebook pages). However, on Facebook, prefectures deliver crisis information that includes – more often – behaviors and specific information on the situation in the territory, compared to the media. As public crisis managers, prefectures are relevant sources of information for populations. It is argued that this quality, more or less constant, is underpinned by the habit of communicating about the crises they manage during a period: this prefecture is prepared to effectively communicate on cyclonic events. In this regard, it seems essential to evaluate the content that organizations disseminate during a crisis, to highlight the good practices at work and suggest ways of improving them systematically. Finally, the importance of having a large number of entry points into the network was stressed, that is, to have a sufficient defined audience basis in order to ensure the effectiveness of the most important crisis communications delivered to protect populations, among other criteria not covered in the example offered. A critical analysis of a real emergency situation (with users' reactions) can constitute an additional review.

7.9. References

Arif, A., Shanahan, K., Chou, F., Dosouto, Y., Starbird, K., and Spiro, E.S. (2016). How information snowballs: exploring the role of exposure in online rumor propagation. *Proceedings of the 19th ACM Conference on Computer-supported Cooperative Work and Social Computing*, 466–477. ACM, New York, USA.

Austin, L., Liu, B.F., and Jin, Y. (2012). How audiences seek out crisis information: Exploring the social-mediated crisis communication model. *J. Appl. Commun. Res.*, 40(2), 188–207. http://doi.org/10.1080/00909882.2012.654498.

Avery, E.J., Graham, M., and Park, S. (2016). Planning makes (closer to) perfect: exploring United States local government officials evaluations of crisis management. *J. Contingencies Crisis Manag.*, 24(2), 73–81.

Berger, J. (2011). Arousal increases social transmission of information. *Assoc. Psychol. Sci.*, 22(7), 891–893. http://doi.org/10.1177/0956797611413294.

Boerman, S.C., Willemsen, L.M., and Van Der Aa, E.P. (2017). "This post is sponsored", effects of sponsorship disclosure on persuasion knowledge and electronic word of mouth in the context of Facebook. *J. Interact. Mark.*, 38, 82–92. http://doi.org/10.1016/j.intmar.2016.12.002.

Coombs, W.T. (2007). *Ongoing Crisis Communication: Planning, Managing, and Responding*. Sage Publications.

Coombs, W.T. and Holladay, S.J. (2010). *The Handbook of Crisis Communication*. John Wiley & Sons.

Coombs, W.T. and Holladay, S.J. (2015). CSR as crisis risk: Expanding how we conceptualize the relationship. *Corp. Comm.: Int. J.*, 20(2), 144–162.

Dedieu, F. (2009). Alerte et catastrophe : le cas de la tempête de 1999, un risque scélérat. *Sociologie Du Travail*, 51(3), 379–401. http://doi.org/10.1016/j.soctra.2009.06.001.

Freberg, K., Saling, K., Vidoloff, K.G., and Eosco, G. (2013). Using value modeling to evaluate social media messages: The case of hurricane Irene. *Public Relat. Rev.*, 39(3), 185–192. http://doi.org/10.1016/j.pubrev.2013.02.010.

Geller, E.S. (1995). Integrating behaviorism and humanism for environmental protection. *J. Soc. Issues*, 51(4), 179–195. http://doi.org/10.1111/j.1540-4560.1995.tb01354.x.

Geller, E.S., Winett, R.A., and Everett, P.B. (1982). *Preserving the Environment: New Strategies for Behavior Change*, 102. Pergamon Press.

Graham, M.W., Avery, E.J., and Park, S. (2015). The role of social media in local government crisis communications. *Public Relat. Rev.*, 41(3), 386–394. http://doi.org/10.1016/j.pubrev.2015.02.001.

Haddow, G.D. and Haddow, K.S. (2014). *Disaster Communications in a Changing Media World*, 2nd edition. Butterworth-Heinemann.

Heimlich, J.E. (2010). Environmental education evaluation: Reinterpreting education as a strategy for meeting mission. *Eval. Program Plann.*, 33, 180–185. http://doi.org/10.1016/j.evalprogplan.2009.07.009.

Houston, J.B., Hawthorne, J., Perreault, M.F., Park, E.H., Hode, M.G., Halliwell, M.R., Turner-McGowen, S.E., Davis, R., Vaid, S., McElderry, J.A., Griffith, S.A. (2014). Social media and disasters: A functional framework for social media use in disaster planning, response, and research. *Disasters*, 39, 1–22. http://doi.org/10.1111/disa.12092.

International Air Transport Association (2014). *Crisis Communications and Social Media: a Best Practice Guide to Communicating in an Emergency*. Available: http://www.iata.org/publications/documents/social-media-crisis-guidelines.pdf.

Johansen, W., Aggerholm, H.K., and Frandsen, F. (2012). Entering new territory: A study of internal crisis management and crisis communication in organizations. *Public Relat. Rev.*, 38(2), 270–279. http://doi.org/10.1016/j.pubrev.2011.11.008.

Keim, M.E. and Noji, E. (2011). Emergent use of social media: A new age of opportunity for disaster resilience. *Am. J. Disaster Med.*, 6(1), 47–54.

Khan, G.F. (2017). *Social Media for Government: A Practical Guide to Understanding, Implementing, and Managing Social Media Tools in the Public Sphere*. Springer. http://doi.org/10.1007/978-981-10-2942-4.

Kim, C. and Yang, S.U. (2017). Like, comment, and share on Facebook: How each behavior differs from the other. *Public Relat. Rev.*, 43(2), 441–449. http://doi.org/10.1016/j.pubrev.2017.02.006.

Lagadec, P. (1991). *La gestion des crises*. Ediscience international, Paris.

Lerchs, M., Mertens, P., Ramacker, B., and Davier, T. (2017). *Alerter pour sauver des vies*. BeAlert. Available: https://crisiscentrum.be/sites/default/files/brochure_alerter_pour_sauver_des_vies_fr_0.pdf.

Mitroff, I.I. (1994). *Crisis Management and Environmentalism: A Natural Fit*. California Management Review, California.

Newman, N., Fletcher, R., Levy, D.A.L., and Rasmus, K.N. (2016). *Reuters Institute Digital News Report 2016*. Reuters Institute for the Study of Journalism, Oxford.

Office of Emergency Management and State Emergency Management Committee (2017). *Emergency Risk Management Local Government Handbook*. Available: https://www.oem.wa.gov.au/Documents/Resources/RiskTools/toolbox/WAERMHandbook2017.pdf.

Omilion-Hodges, L.M. and McClain, K.L. (2016). University use of social media and the crisis lifecycle: Organizational messages, first information responders' reactions, reframed messages and dissemination patterns. *Comput. Hum. Behav.*, 54, 630–638.

Palttala, P. and Vos, M. (2012). Quality indicators for crisis communication to support emergency management by public authorities. *J. Conting. Crisis Man.*, 20(1), 39–51. http://doi.org/10.1111/j.1468-5973.2011.00654.x.

Parmer, J., Baur, C., Eroglu, D., Lubell, K., Prue, C., Reynolds, B., and Weaver, J. (2016). Crisis and emergency risk messaging in mass media news stories: Is the public getting the information they need to protect their health? *Health Commun.*, 236(March), 1–8. http://doi.org/10.1080/10410236.2015.1049728.

Rowe, G. and Frewer, L.J. (2005). A typology of public engagement mechanisms. *Sci. Technol. Hum. Val.*, 30(2), 251–290. http://doi.org/10.1177/0162243904271724.

Schultz, P.W. (2010). Making energy conservation the norm. In *People-centered Initiatives for Focusing Energy Savings*, Ehrhardt-Martinez, K. and Laitner, J. (eds). ACEEE, Washington, DC.

Schultz, P.W. (2014). Strategies for Promoting Proenvironmental Behavior: Lots of Tools but Few Instructions. *Eur. Psychol.*, 19(2), 107–117. http://doi.org/10.1027/1016-9040/a000163.

Schwarzenegger, A. (2004). *Local Government Emergency Planning Handbook*. Available: http://www.energy.ca.gov/emergencies/documents /2004-03-11_GOV_EMRGNCY_HNDB.PDF.

Seeger, M.W. (2006). Best practices in crisis communication: An expert panel process. *J. Appl. Commun. Res.*, 34(3), 232–244. http://doi.org/10.1080/00909880600769944

Steelman, T.A., McCaffrey, S.M., Velez, A.K., and Briefel, J.A. (2015). What information do people use, trust, and find useful. *Nat Hazards*, 76(1), 615–634. http://doi.org/10.1007/s11069-014-1512-x.

Valls, M., Cazeneuve, B., Christiane, T., Sapin, M., Le Drian, J.-Y., and Paul-Langevin, G. (2014a). Décret n° 2014-1253 du 27 octobre 2014 relatif aux dispositions des livres III, VI et VII de la partie réglementaire du code de la sécurité intérieure (Décrets en Conseil d'Etat et décrets simples) – Article R732-19. In *Code de la sécurité intérieure*. Available: https://www.legifrance.gouv.fr/eli/decret/2014/10/27/INTD1401671D/jo/article_r732-19.

Valls, M., Cazeneuve, B., Christiane, T., Sapin, M., Le Drian, J.-Y., and Paul-Langevin, G. (2014b). Décret n° 2014-1253 du 27 octobre 2014 relatif aux dispositions des livres III, VI et VII de la partie réglementaire du code de la sécurité intérieure (Décrets en Conseil d'Etat et décrets simples) – Article R732-20. In *Code de la sécurité intérieure*. Available: https://www.legifrance.gouv.fr/affichCodeArticle.do?cidTexte=LEGITE XT000025503132&idArticle=LEGIARTI000029657032&dateTexte=&c ategorieLien=cid

van der Meer, T.G.L.A., Verhoeven, P., Beentjes, H.W.J., and Vliegenthart, R. (2017). Communication in times of crisis: The stakeholder relationship under pressure. *Public Relat. Rev.*, 43(2), 426–440. https://doi.org/10.1016/j.pubrev.2017.02.005.

Wang, Y., Zeng, D.D., Zhu, B., Xiaolong, Z., and Wang, F. (2012). Patterns of news dissemination through online news media: A case study in China. *Inform. Syst. Front.*, 16, 557–570. http://doi.org/10.1007 /s10796-012-9358-9.

8

Some Perspectives Moving Forward

8.1. Introduction

The most severe part of a crisis is the most difficult phase for decision makers to face because the environment is dynamic and unstable, forcing crisis units to operate in degraded conditions. The fragilities that can appear within a crisis unit expose it to several types of disturbances. The rush of events, the massive arrival of information, sometimes incomplete or contradictory, and the need to report in a public way on the actions taken are just a few examples. These factors can thus destabilize the members of a crisis unit. Faced with emergency decision-making, they must nevertheless continue to carry out their missions and implement appropriate measures and means to protect the people, property and environment affected by the event.

In order to better understand the difficulties that reduce its effectiveness, it is necessary to understand the composition and functioning of a strategic crisis unit. A crisis unit goes beyond the status of a simple "group" described as an ephemeral organization. The crisis unit's strong organizational integration requires a high

Chapter written by Sophie SAUVAGNARGUES, Dimitri LAPIERRE, Philippe LIMOUSIN, Noémie FRÉALLE, Florian TENA-CHOLLET, David GOUTX, Pierre-Alain AYRAL, Aurélia BONY-DANDRIEUX and Jérôme TIXIER.

capacity to adapt to an unknown situation, while its members assume various roles and responsibilities that are finely structured and hierarchical. The members of a crisis unit are mobilized according to the skills and knowledge they possess to achieve their missions. While the need to carry out the tasks assigned to them is essential today, it is also necessary to note the importance attached to the various teamwork processes to achieve this. The analysis of different behavioral, cognitive and motivational processes allows us to stress the importance of "teamwork" in a team that pursues common objectives, whatever the function of each one may be. The influence of the group on decision-making, the existence of strongly involved sensitive issues, a temporal pressure, or even political problems associated with the representation of the situation as well as a whole set of cognitive biases degrade the entire process, from the perception of the situation to decision-making.

Today, it is therefore necessary that crisis managers are trained and that crisis management training sessions fully correspond to the needs identified. This requirement is justified by regulatory constraints, and it is also fundamental that decision makers gain experience and strengthen their levels of expertise. Among other things, training must allow for the reduction of dysfunctions identified at the collective and individual levels which occur in crisis units.

Retrospective analysis of these difficulties encountered by decision makers and their teams during strategic crisis management highlights the positive impact of the experience on the processes of coordination, shared mental representation, organization of intergroup behavior and decision-making. The need to set up training exercises is therefore based on the importance of reproducing specific complex and uncertain, urgent and unknown, catastrophic and destabilizing situations in the long term.

Research results (Tena-Chollet 2012; Lapierre 2016; Limousin 2017; Fréalle 2018) have highlighted the importance of the decision maker and their team's ability to perform crisis management strategies by integrating their feedback into scenarios reproducing the conditions and situations with which they have already been confronted. It is imperative for the decision maker and their team to be able to maintain an optimal level of involvement and mobilization of key crisis management skills during exercises simulating unforeseen or unknown events inherent in any major crisis.

To integrate these research results, a simulator was used as a support, which is a real semi-virtual training environment for strategic crisis management. This environment is based on a design methodology that uses a triple temporal-system-functional approach aimed at characterizing the essential components and interactions expected from a training platform.

Within this research platform, it is thus possible to develop and test different facilities, and to immerse trainees in crisis situations by isolating them in a room and reestablishing the a crisis unit.

Works on crisis management training have shown that the preparation, organization, animation and retrospective analysis of exercises are characterized by difficulties and problems related not only to the problem concerned but also to the inadequacy of the technical–pedagogical framework with respect to the profiles and needs of participants.

The review of knowledge in terms of organizational learning and teaching environment has also allowed the identification of perspectives and ways of improvement, in terms of both realistic simulation of a crisis scenario and optimization of the teaching processes involved and of the tools implemented.

8.2. Understanding what is played out in a crisis unit

8.2.1. *From the observation and debriefing point of view*

The consideration of human and organizational factors and the formalization of the evaluation during crisis management training allows us to propose a relevant observation of what plays out during a training and thus to produce an analysis by debriefing on the performances of learners during exercises.

Based on this situation, an EVADE (Evaluation and Debriefing Assistance) evaluation method has been developed, which simultaneously integrates the technical and non-technical expectations of a crisis unit and is applicable on a collective scale (Lapierre 2016). This innovative method proposes to carry out an evaluation in real time, with two main objectives: to make the training courses more immersive and dynamic (by adapting the scenario and requesting skills according to the choices chosen by learners) and to be an aid to debriefing.

In order to move forward, this evaluation methodology and debriefing assistance would require establishing the educational reference framework created (voluntarily generic and transposable) with different organizations. It would be interesting to propose an initial in-depth assessment of the skills of learners who need to participate in crisis management training. This pre-assessment could include a mapping of learners' skills before training in order to identify the benefits. It could take the form of individual questionnaires or interviews, specific to the crisis management organization and to the functions that members perform through their respective sub-units. This would allow evaluators to focus and select the instructional objectives of exercises. During a simulation, they could then verify the mobilization, acquisition, development and/or consolidation of the identified skills.

Moreover, integrating this type of methodology into a training plan would allow for a follow-up within the organization of several exercises to evaluate the progress margin of the members of the crisis unit throughout their learning process. The skill-based approach as well as the gradation aspect symbolized by the three difficulty levels (beginner, intermediate and expert) would be interesting in this case.

8.2.2. *From the physiological and behavioral point of view*

The human organism is a set of systems regulated and interconnected in order to adapt to environmental stimuli. Thus, when performing a task, the nervous system stores relevant information, plans a response and then activates and regulates the functioning of the muscular system. As a result, the cardiovascular system, more intensely stressed, adjusts its components. In particular, it has been shown that during a cognitive task, the increase in cognitive load leads to the modulation of each of these systems. Indeed, an increase in heart rate and a decrease in its variability have been observed (Matthews *et al.* 2015). In brain imaging, an increase in signal amplitude at the prefrontal level (Ayaz *et al.* 2012) and frequency modulation at the centro-parietal and occipital levels have been observed (Käthner *et al.* 2014; Causse *et al.* 2015).

In the context of crisis management, it is essential to have tools that offer the possibility of optimizing operators' performance. Indeed, in this type of situation, the stressful context and the important stakes add many parameters that amplify the biological limits of the operator, as in the case of attentional blink (Dehais *et al.* 2014). Recent studies (Aghajani and Omurtag 2016) have suggested that the combination of several physiological data would allow better decoding of physiological signatures of cognitive load.

It would therefore be relevant to develop devices (biomedical, psychosensory, home automation, voice, indoor location, etc.) using a multi-domain approach to observe or characterize behavioral processes, cognitive and motivational measures of individuals subjected to decision-making in emergency situations and in confined environments, such as crisis units, and an analytical method for combining these measures to identify a physiological signature of increased workload in working memory. This approach, currently being developed as part of an interdisciplinary project (a collaboration between EUROMOV University of Montpellier and IMT Mines Alès-LGI2P-Institut des Sciences des Risques), is used in many fields such as behavioral neurosciences, neuropsychology, artificial learning, transfer learning, rehabilitation medicine, risk sciences and major crisis management. The use of crisis management training sessions is a testing ground in this particularly innovative field.

8.3. Developing new methods to improve learner immersion

8.3.1. *Getting closer to reality, or modifying it*

Knowledge of the simulated phenomenon during the exercise is a necessary precondition for the construction of the crisis management exercise. It is possible to use feedback from major past events in order to study the phenomenon via modeling. If this feedback brings positive realism to the simulation (it has happened!), it can lead to a bias during the exercise by calling upon the memory of "players". This is the case, for example, when working on cyclonic risk, where it is possible for some players to recognize the cyclone "played" very early in the simulation by observing the characteristics presented during the simulation. In this context, modeling can be an important means of generating an "unprecedented" event and its associated consequences (Ayral *et al.* 2018).

If modeling is used before the simulation, the gain could also be important if it were possible to use it during the simulation. Indeed, during the crisis management exercise, the elements related to the phenomenon in the scenario are generally "rigid", and consequences or disruptive events serve as adjustment variables for the facilitator. Aggravating or reducing the intensity of a phenomenon during the simulation and the associated consequences could therefore constitute an important advantage for the facilitator. For example, during a flood scenario, it would be a matter of increasing the amount of rainfall and of generating the consequences in terms of flow, floodplain area and water levels. This could also be the increase in the wind in the event of forest fire, the importance of a leak in case of a gas release, the height of the swell and so on.

The computation times of physical and numerical models required to perform these simulations make it impossible to use them in the crisis management exercise context. Several avenues of research can be evoked: (1) developing a modeling scenario before the crisis management exercise or (2) using metamodels based on statistical approaches (neural networks, for example), which will, by learning, simulate the functioning of the physical model with a significant gain in computation times. Generating several scenarios upstream of the simulation with a model and using a metamodel during the simulation are two levers that should be explored considerably in further research.

8.3.2. Encouraging learner engagement

Serious games are devices that can help improve the truth of the learner's position.

They associate a serious objective with a game (Szilas 2007), and are used in various fields such as defense, health and education (Bellino and Colombi 2012). Their educational scope is actually in their definition: they are playful. They enable potential learning to be made effective as learning, as a complement to the selection of educational objectives used in developing a learning situation. The game reinforces the commitment of the player in their experience, and the implementation of the mechanics of scripting used in serious games (interactive narration) is an interesting research track, because during the "classic" scripting of a crisis exercise, the designer must choose between the coherence of the story and the freedom of characters, and try to establish a multilinear scenario. Interactive narration makes it possible to implement methodologies to adapt to the learner's choice, while maintaining the guideline of the scenario.

The analogy between the "classic" crisis scenario and interactive narration allows us to envisage research avenues (Fréalle 2018), in order to produce a methodology that allows the scenario to evolve despite potentially unpredictable choices of learners, constrain the game world to limit the participants' options, offer the tools to the master of animation to orchestrate the scenario, allow the scenario to evolve during the exercise and give the facilitators the opportunity to share their given elements during the scenario.

Learning becomes more effective in an openly playful setting, through a reinforced engagement via the game's mechanisms. However, it is also possible to reach a certain depth of engagement, a true awareness of responsibility, when play takes hold of a seemingly serious training.

Ludicity is the part of the game inherent in the simulation of crisis management, and by exploiting its intrinsic mechanisms, it is possible to enrich the simulation without distorting its nature as a pedagogical exercise. In particular, beyond the learning of skills by their use in a situation quite close to reality, it is possible to give the simulation an emotional consistency, bringing its content even closer to the complexity of the experience lived in a real-world crisis management environment. This is what we have referred to as a high-resolution simulation.

A classical approach tends to spontaneously consider that reality is factual and true and that a simulation should approach it as far as possible. However, along with Baudrillard (1981), we can question this relationship of simulation with reality. Indeed, for the vast majority of people summoned to a real crisis room (apart from professionals such as the military and firefighters), experiences of crisis management are often limited to the idea that these exercises show how to behave correctly in a crisis situation. The simulation then comes as an extra layer of preparation that provides a fictitious baseline experience to which the future crisis manager will conform when plunged into real crisis management. In other words, real crisis management is not simply reaching the truth of what the simulation tries to approach, but perhaps the final stage of the simulation becomes the reality, which Baudrillard refers to as the simulacrum.

In this game of mirrors between simulation, simulacrum and reality, what ultimately matters is the truth of the participant's position in the simulation, and the lucidity of the way they look at what the Ludicity of the simulation reveals of their behavior and their ability, ultimately, to assume the responsibility that falls to them.

8.3.3. *Developing credible, pedagogical and interactive exercise scenarios*

Implementing training involves providing an effective learning situation. It is necessary to set a number of pedagogical objectives that learners can achieve, to choose among the possible types of training the one that is best suited, and, when implementing training, it is essential to put in place elements that promote learning so that the learner is motivated and committed to learning.

The implementation of a simulation requires the development of a scenario whose success criteria are credibility, pedagogical scope and interactivity. In its preparation, the implementation of these criteria should be ensured. This implies a certain number of pedagogical choices (selection of the hazard, the type of crisis unit, etc.) and design choices (self-powered or controlled scenario structure, writing of the timeline, etc.) that are made before the exercise is carried out.

Interactivity criteria are essential during the execution of the scenario, and at present, there are few methods to integrate it into the exercise. The encouraging contributions of system engineering to automating the construction of crisis scenarios thus make it possible to present all the concepts and elements of scenario development, taking into account their possible interactions (Limousin *et al.* 2016). The methods used to facilitate crisis exercises are also of interest and, more specifically, the improvement of interactions between facilitators and learners in order to adapt the scenario to their reactions during the exercise. Modeling the circulation of information between learners and facilitators, and within the facilitators, makes it possible to propose a set of participative devices (collaborative map, animation handrail, facilitator situation points, etc.) that will contribute to maintaining a high level of interactivity during the exercise (Fréalle *et al.* 2017).

8.4. Implementing innovative complementary tools

Within the simulation and research platform of the Institut des Sciences des Risques (IMT Mines Alès), a software tool called TwitterLike was developed to simulate the media pressure on social networks, with an operation based on the Twitter platform. Based on a Twitter API and developed with web technologies (PHP language), TwitterLike is hosted on an IMT Mines Alès server and is accessible from the outside, which allows remote use (Pot 2015).

TwitterLike works as follows. Facilitators can endorse the identity of any actor or person involved in the crisis scenario and can thus send messages of different types (text only, text with photo) and nature (certified information, rumor, inaccurate information, etc.). The opportunity to load pre-recorded messages can make it easier to send messages when they are part of the scenario itself. The participants in the exercise (the crisis unit) assume the role of the mobilized organization (a local community, for example) and can implement its crisis communication strategy by responding (or not) to the messages that pass through and being proactive by passing instructions or denying rumors if they so wish.

During a TwitterLike simulation, the tool can retrieve tweets on Twitter in real time (if the option is enabled) and inject them into the TwitterLike message thread. This possibility makes users aware of the need to sort and prioritize the information received.

However, any message exchanged during a TwitterLike simulation remains limited to the TwitterLike tool, and is therefore not published on Twitter. A database is used to store the tweets exchanged in order to offer the possibility of post-exercise analysis.

This tool therefore makes it possible to raise awareness of the use of social media for emergency management, and several perspectives can be mentioned.

First of all, the enrichment of TwitterLike with eponymous social network features would contribute to making the simulation more realistic and to proposing real crisis communication training.

Finally, a transposition toward other useful or used social networks in crisis situations is envisaged. The development of a FacebookLike tool could, for example, make it possible to raise awareness of crisis communication among other types of public social networks not covered by a Twitter-type network.

8.5. Conclusion

Crisis management training is increasingly deployed within state or private organizations in order to better prepare decision makers to face potential crises.

Research on the subject is developing in parallel with the growing power of needs. In the chapters of this book, advances relating to the various phases of creation and realization of an exercise have been presented. It is also important to set out some research perspectives for the coming years.

Two main axes can be summarized from this perspective:

1) To increase the flexibility and realism of the scenarios in order to open up to more interactive, innovative and playful exercises for learners. This must involve the creation of more interactive scenarios that integrate participants' skills and needs as closely as possible. The issue is the immersion of learners in scenarios, which must be increased so that learning improves.

2) To improve the individual's physiological knowledge, and also that of a group subjected to strong constraints to better observe, evaluate and restore "the gain in knowledge, skills and abilities" acquired during a crisis simulation exercise. This knowledge should then be translated into practical tools for trainers to improve the debriefing phase that is essential for learning.

If it is now possible to create and execute scenarios by integrating essential prerequisites, it remains, however, essential that this be integrated into a continuous improvement process. This is in order to make crisis management exercises ever more effective and thus make them real areas for experimentation in the field of decision support systems in crisis situations.

8.6. References

Aghajani, H., and Omurtag, A. (2016). Assessment of mental workload by EEG+ fNIRS. *Engineering in Medicine and Biology Society (EMBC), 2016 IEEE 38th Annual International Conference of the IEEE*, August, pp. 3773–3776.

Ayaz, H., Shewokis, P.A., Bunce, S., Izzetoglu, K., Willems, B., and Onaral, B. (2012). Optical brain monitoring for operator training and mental workload assessment. *Neuroimage*, 59(1), 36–47.

Ayral, P.-A., Fréalle, N., Sauvagnargues, S., Téna-Chollet, F., Agon, P., Amourdom, P., Bonnardot, F., Bousquet, O., Germain, M.-C., Hibon, P., Ivoula, J., Lecacheux, S., Meister, J., Paris, F., Pesnel, E., Quetelard, H., and Recouvreur, R. (2018). Exercices de gestion de crise à l'échelle communale en contexte cyclonique – Application aux communes de Saint-Paul et Sainte-Suzanne, *14ème Rencontre annuelle Géorisque*, Montpellier.

Baudrillard, J. (1981), *Simulacres et simulations*. Galilée, Paris.

Bellino, C. and Colombi, T. (2012). Jouer pour apprendre : vers une ergonomie "ludopédagogique". *Colloques scientifiques SEGAMED*. Nice.

Causse, M., Fabre, E., Giraudet, L., Gonzalez, M., and Peysakhovich, V. (2015). EEG/ERP as a measure of mental workload in a simple piloting task. *Procedia Manufacturing*, 3, 5230–5236.

Dehais, F., Causse, M., Vachon, F., Régis, N., Menant, E., and Tremblay, S. (2014). Failure to detect critical auditory alerts in the cockpit: evidence for inattentional deafness. *Hum. Factors*, 56(4), 631–644.

Fréalle, N., Tena-Chollet, F., and Sauvagnargues, S. (2017). The animation in the execution of crisis management exercises. In *Proceedings of the 14th International Conference on Information Systems for Crisis Response and Management: Agility if Coming*, Comes, T., Bénaben, F., Hanachi, C., Lauras, M., and Montarnal, A. (eds). ISCRAM, Albi..

Fréalle, N. (2018). Formation à la gestion de crise à l'échelle communale : méthode d'élaboration et de mise en oeuvre de scénarios de crise crédibles, pédagogiques et interactifs. PhD Thesis, University of St-Etienne.

Käthner, I., Wriessnegger, S.C., Müller-Putz, G.R., Kübler, A., and Halder, S. (2014). Effects of mental workload and fatigue on the P300, alpha and theta band power during operation of an ERP (P300) brain–computer interface. *Biol. Psychol.*, 102, 118–129.

Lapierre, D., (2016). Méthode EVADE : Une approche intégrée pour l'EValuation et l'Aide au DEbriefing. PhD Thesis, University of Nîmes.

Limousin P., Tixier J., Bony-Dandieux A., Chapurlat V., and Sauvagnargues S., (2016). A new method and tools to scenarios design for crisis management exercises. *Chem. Eng. Trans.*, 53, 319–324.

Limousin P., (2017). Contribution à la scénarisation pédagogique d'exercices de crise, PhD Thesis, Saint-Etienne School of Mines, Saint-Etienne.

Matthews, G., Reinerman-Jones, L.E., Barber, D.J., and Abich IV, J. (2015). The psychometrics of mental workload: multiple measures are sensitive but divergent. *Hum. Factors*, 57(1), 125–143.

Pot, M. (2015). Développement d'un outil de simulation d'un réseau social pour la formation à la gestion de crise. IUT Montpellier-Sète.

Szilas, N. (2007). A Computational model of an intelligent narrator for interactive narratives. *Appl. Artif. Intell.*, 21(8), 753–801. doi: 10.1080/08839510701526574.

Tena-Chollet, F. (2012). Elaboration d'un environnement semi-virtuel de formation à la gestion stratégique de crise, basé sur la simulation multi-agents. PhD Thesis, Saint-Etienne School of Mines, Saint-Etienne.

List of Authors

Pierre-Alain AYRAL
LGEI – Institute of Risk
Sciences
IMT Mines Alès
University of Montpellier
France

Aurélia BONY-DANDRIEUX
LGEI – Institute of Risk
Sciences
IMT Mines Alès
University of Montpellier
France

Serge CAPAROS
Laboratoire CHROME
University of Nîmes
France

Noémie FRÉALLE
LGEI – Institute of Risk
Sciences
IMT Mines Alès
University of Montpellier
France

David GOUTX
LGEI – Institute of Risk
Sciences
IMT Mines Alès
University of Montpellier
France

Dimitri LAPIERRE
LGEI – Institute of Risk
Sciences
IMT Mines Alès
University of Montpellier
France

Clément LAVERDET
Laboratoire CHROME
University of Nîmes
France

Philippe LIMOUSIN
LGEI – Institute of Risk
Sciences
IMT Mines Alès
University of Montpellier
France

Laurent MERMET
Centre International de
Recherche sur
l'Environnement et le
Développement
AgroParisTech
Paris
France

Sophie SAUVAGNARGUES
LGEI – Institute of Risk
Sciences
IMT Mines Alès
University of Montpellier
France

Florian TENA-CHOLLET
LGEI – Institute of Risk
Sciences
IMT Mines Alès
University of Montpellier
France

Jérôme TIXIER
LGEI – Institute of Risk
Sciences
IMT Mines Alès
University of Montpellier
France

Karine WEISS
Laboratoire CHROME
University of Nîmes
France

Index

Other titles from

in

Information Systems, Web and Pervasive Computing

2018

ARDUIN Pierre-Emmanuel
Insider Threats
(Advances in Information Systems Set – Volume 10)

CHAMOUX Jean-Pierre
The Digital Era 1: Big Data Stakes

CARMÈS Maryse
Digital Organizations Manufacturing: Scripts, Performativity and Semiopolitics
(Intellectual Technologies Set – Volume 5)

DOUAY Nicolas
Urban Planning in the Digital Age
(Intellectual Technologies Set – Volume 6)

FABRE Renaud, BENSOUSSAN Alain
The Digital Factory for Knowledge: Production and Validation of Scientific Results

GAUDIN Thierry, LACROIX Dominique, MAUREL Marie-Christine, POMEROL Jean-Charles
Life Sciences, Information Sciences

GAYARD Laurent
Darknet: Geopolitics and Uses
(Computing and Connected Society Set – Volume 2)

IAFRATE Fernando
Artificial Intelligence and Big Data: The Birth of a New Intelligence
(Advances in Information Systems Set – Volume 8)

LE DEUFF Olivier
Digital Humanities: History and Development
(Intellectual Technologies Set – Volume 4)

MANDRAN Nadine
Traceable Human Experiment Design Research: Theoretical Model and Practical Guide
(Advances in Information Systems Set – Volume 9)

PIVERT Olivier
NoSQL Data Models: Trends and Challenges

ROCHET Claude
Smart Cities: Reality or Fiction

SEDKAOUI Soraya
Data Analytics and Big Data

SZONIECKY Samuel
Ecosystems Knowledge: Modeling and Analysis Method for Information and Communication
(Digital Tools and Uses Set – Volume 6)

2017

BOUHAÏ Nasreddine, SALEH Imad
Internet of Things: Evolutions and Innovations
(Digital Tools and Uses Set – Volume 4)

DUONG Véronique
Baidu SEO: Challenges and Intricacies of Marketing in China

LESAS Anne-Marie, MIRANDA Serge
The Art and Science of NFC Programming
(Intellectual Technologies Set – Volume 3)

LIEM André
Prospective Ergonomics
(Human-Machine Interaction Set – Volume 4)

MARSAULT Xavier
Eco-generative Design for Early Stages of Architecture
(Architecture and Computer Science Set – Volume 1)

REYES-GARCIA Everardo
The Image-Interface: Graphical Supports for Visual Information
(Digital Tools and Uses Set – Volume 3)

REYES-GARCIA Everardo, BOUHAÏ Nasreddine
Designing Interactive Hypermedia Systems
(Digital Tools and Uses Set – Volume 2)

SAÏD Karim, BAHRI KORBI Fadia
Asymmetric Alliances and Information Systems:Issues and Prospects
(Advances in Information Systems Set – Volume 7)

SZONIECKY Samuel, BOUHAÏ Nasreddine
*Collective Intelligence and Digital Archives: Towards Knowledge
Ecosystems*
(Digital Tools and Uses Set – Volume 1)

2016

BEN CHOUIKHA Mona
Organizational Design for Knowledge Management

BERTOLO David
Interactions on Digital Tablets in the Context of 3D Geometry Learning
(Human-Machine Interaction Set – Volume 2)

BOUVARD Patricia, SUZANNE Hervé
Collective Intelligence Development in Business

EL FALLAH SEGHROUCHNI Amal, ISHIKAWA Fuyuki, HÉRAULT Laurent, TOKUDA Hideyuki
Enablers for Smart Cities

FABRE Renaud, in collaboration with MESSERSCHMIDT-MARIET Quentin, HOLVOET Margot
New Challenges for Knowledge

GAUDIELLO Ilaria, ZIBETTI Elisabetta
Learning Robotics, with Robotics, by Robotics
(Human-Machine Interaction Set – Volume 3)

HENROTIN Joseph
The Art of War in the Network Age
(Intellectual Technologies Set – Volume 1)

KITAJIMA Munéo
Memory and Action Selection in Human–Machine Interaction
(Human–Machine Interaction Set – Volume 1)

LAGRAÑA Fernando
E-mail and Behavioral Changes: Uses and Misuses of Electronic Communications

LEIGNEL Jean-Louis, UNGARO Thierry, STAAR Adrien
Digital Transformation
(Advances in Information Systems Set – Volume 6)

NOYER Jean-Max
Transformation of Collective Intelligences
(Intellectual Technologies Set – Volume 2)

VENTRE Daniel
Information Warfare – 2nd edition

VITALIS André
The Uncertain Digital Revolution
(Computing and Connected Society Set – Volume 1)

KEMBELLEC Gérald, CHARTRON Ghislaine, SALEH Imad
Recommender Systems

MATHIAN Hélène, SANDERS Lena
Spatio-temporal Approaches: Geographic Objects and Change Process

PLANTIN Jean-Christophe
Participatory Mapping

VENTRE Daniel
Chinese Cybersecurity and Defense

2013

BERNIK Igor
Cybercrime and Cyberwarfare

CAPET Philippe, DELAVALLADE Thomas
Information Evaluation

LEBRATY Jean-Fabrice, LOBRE-LEBRATY Katia
Crowdsourcing: One Step Beyond

SALLABERRY Christian
Geographical Information Retrieval in Textual Corpora

2012

BUCHER Bénédicte, LE BER Florence
Innovative Software Development in GIS

GAUSSIER Eric, YVON François
Textual Information Access

STOCKINGER Peter
Audiovisual Archives: Digital Text and Discourse Analysis

VENTRE Daniel
Cyber Conflict

2011

BANOS Arnaud, THÉVENIN Thomas
Geographical Information and Urban Transport Systems

DAUPHINÉ André
Fractal Geography

LEMBERGER Pirmin, MOREL Mederic
Managing Complexity of Information Systems

STOCKINGER Peter
Introduction to Audiovisual Archives

STOCKINGER Peter
Digital Audiovisual Archives

VENTRE Daniel
Cyberwar and Information Warfare

2010

BONNET Pierre
Enterprise Data Governance

BRUNET Roger
Sustainable Geography

CARREGA Pierre
Geographical Information and Climatology

CAUVIN Colette, ESCOBAR Francisco, SERRADJ Aziz
Thematic Cartography – 3-volume series
Thematic Cartography and Transformations – Volume 1
Cartography and the Impact of the Quantitative Revolution – Volume 2
New Approaches in Thematic Cartography – Volume 3

LANGLOIS Patrice
Simulation of Complex Systems in GIS

MATHIS Philippe
Graphs and Networks – 2nd edition

THERIAULT Marius, DES ROSIERS François
Modeling Urban Dynamics

2009

BONNET Pierre, DETAVERNIER Jean-Michel, VAUQUIER Dominique
Sustainable IT Architecture: the Progressive Way of Overhauling Information Systems with SOA

PAPY Fabrice
Information Science

RIVARD François, ABOU HARB Georges, MERET Philippe
The Transverse Information System

ROCHE Stéphane, CARON Claude
Organizational Facets of GIS

2008

BRUGNOT Gérard
Spatial Management of Risks

FINKE Gerd
Operations Research and Networks

GUERMOND Yves
Modeling Process in Geography

KANEVSKI Michael
Advanced Mapping of Environmental Data

MANOUVRIER Bernard, LAURENT Ménard
Application Integration: EAI, B2B, BPM and SOA

PAPY Fabrice
Digital Libraries

2007

DOBESCH Hartwig, DUMOLARD Pierre, DYRAS Izabela
Spatial Interpolation for Climate Data

SANDERS Lena
Models in Spatial Analysis

2006

CLIQUET Gérard
Geomarketing

CORNIOU Jean-Pierre
Looking Back and Going Forward in IT

DEVILLERS Rodolphe, JEANSOULIN Robert
Fundamentals of Spatial Data Quality

Printed and bound by CPI Group (UK) Ltd, Croydon, CR0 4YY